*a guide to* ARTIFICIAL INTELLIGENCE
*with* VISUAL PROLOG

*a guide to* ARTIFICIAL INTELLIGENCE
*with* VISUAL PROLOG

RANDALL SCOTT

**Outskirts Press, Inc.
Denver, Colorado**

The opinions expressed in this manuscript are solely the opinions of the author and do not represent the opinions or thoughts of the publisher. The author has represented and warranted full ownership and/or legal right to publish all the materials in this book.

A Guide to Artificial Intelligence with Visual Prolog
All Rights Reserved.
Copyright © 2010 Randall Scott
v3.0

Visual Prolog
All rights reserved – used with permission
Copyright © 1984-2009, Prolog Development Center A/S.

Cover Photo © 2010 JupiterImages Corporation. All rights reserved - used with permission.

This book may not be reproduced, transmitted, or stored in whole or in part by any means, including graphic, electronic, or mechanical without the express written consent of the publisher except in the case of brief quotations embodied in critical articles and reviews.

Outskirts Press, Inc.
http://www.outskirtspress.com

ISBN: 978-1-4327-4936-1

Outskirts Press and the "OP" logo are trademarks belonging to Outskirts Press, Inc.

PRINTED IN THE UNITED STATES OF AMERICA

# Contents

Acknowledgements ................................................................. ix
Introduction ........................................................................... xi
The Prolog Language ............................................................. 1
   1.1 How Prolog fits into Artificial Intelligence ....................... 1
   1.2 Prolog Basics and General Information ......................... 2
   1.3 Summary ...................................................................... 10
Visual Prolog ......................................................................... 13
   2.1 For Beginners ............................................................... 13
      2.1.1 How to Download and Install ............................. 13
      2.1.2 Orientation – How and where to look for Help .... 15
      2.1.3 Tutorials ............................................................. 20
      2.1.4 The Prolog Inference Engine (PIE) ....................... 20
   2.2 Past the Beginner Mode .............................................. 22
      2.2.1 Scoping ............................................................... 22
      2.2.2 Database Environment ....................................... 24
      2.2.3 The Integrated Development Environment ......... 26
      2.2.4 Application Development .................................... 26

  2.2.5 Other useful Commercial Application Features ..... 27
  2.2.6 Prolog Classic Examples ................................... 28
**Sample Application** ................................................................**33**
 3.1 Application Discussion ................................................ 33
 3.2 Application Design Considerations ............................. 33
 3.3 Incremental Programming ........................................... 35
  3.3.1 Starting Data ...................................................... 35
  3.3.2 Data Importing .................................................. 37
  3.3.3 Piecing together the Application Source Code ...... 39
   3.3.3.1 Creating a Package for specific
   Functionality ........................................................ 42
   3.3.3.2 Polishing Visual Prolog
   generated GUI items ........................................... 44
   3.3.3.3 Organizing our Functional Source Code ...... 49
   3.3.3.4 Import Data .................................................. 54
   3.3.3.5 Data Analysis ............................................... 63
   3.3.3.6 Producing Results ......................................... 69
   3.3.3.7 Clean up ...................................................... 76
   3.3.3.8 Finishing Touches .......................................... 84
   3.3.3.8.7 About Dialog ............................................. 130
 3.4 Incremental Programming Road Map ......................... 132
 3.5 Summary .................................................................. 133
**References** ............................................................................**137**
 4.1 Built-in Predicates .................................................... 137
 4.2 Program Foundation Class (PFC) ............................... 138
 4.3 Help Avenues .......................................................... 140
  4.3.1 Built in Help ..................................................... 141
  4.3.2 PDC Resources on the Web .............................. 142
   4.3.2.1 Language Reference Wiki ........................... 143

- 4.3.2.2 Knowledge Base ........................................ 144
- 4.3.2.3 Tutorials ................................................... 145
- 4.3.2.4 Discussion Forum ....................................... 147
- 4.4 Source Code for Sample Application ........................ 147
  - 4.4.1 LottoDomains.cl ................................................ 148
  - 4.4.2 LottoDomains.pro .............................................. 149
  - 4.4.3 ConvertData.cl ................................................. 150
  - 4.4.4 ConvertData.pro ............................................... 150
  - 4.4.5 GetNumbers.cl ................................................. 161
  - 4.4.6 GetNumbers.pro ............................................... 162
  - 4.4.7 Numbers.cl ...................................................... 166
  - 4.4.8 Numbers.i ....................................................... 167
  - 4.4.9 Numbers.pro .................................................... 167
  - 4.4.10 Help.cl ......................................................... 170
  - 4.4.11 Help.i .......................................................... 171
  - 4.4.12 Help.pro ....................................................... 171
  - 4.4.13 HelpWindow.cl ............................................... 172
  - 4.4.14 HelpWindow.pro ............................................. 173
  - 4.4.15 TaskWindow.pro ............................................. 174
  - 4.4.16 ImportInstructions.hlp ...................................... 177

# List of Figures

2.1.2.a - IDE Help Menu ....................................................... 16
2.1.2.b - IDE Web Help Menu ................................................ 17
2.1.4 - PIE ............................................................................. 21
3.3.2.a - Create Project GAMegaLotto (Personal Edition View) .. 40
3.3.2.b - Project Tree (Commercial Edition View) ...................... 42
3.3.3.2 - TaskMenu Menu GUI Editor ..................................... 48
3.3.3.5 - Visual Prolog Break Point and Debug ....................... 68
3.3.3.8.2 - Numbers Form ..................................................... 102
3.3.3.8.6.a - Create a Separate Window Object ................... 124
3.3.3.8.6.b(1) - Application View [Import + Numbers] ........... 128
3.3.3.8.6.b(2) - Application View [Help] ................................ 129
3.3.3.8.7 - About Dialog ..................................................... 131
3.4 - Predicate Call Visibility ................................................ 134
4.3.1 - Visual Prolog Help .................................................. 141
4.3.2 - Visual Prolog Tutorials ............................................. 142
4.3.2.1 - Language Reference Wiki ...................................... 143
4.3.2.2 - Knowledge Base ................................................... 144
4.3.2.3.a – Beginners' Guide to Visual Prolog (PDC Web) ...... 145
4.3.2.3.b - Visual Prolog for Tyros (PDC Web) ...................... 146
4.3.2.4 – Visual Prolog Discussion Forum ............................ 147

# Acknowledgements

I would like to acknowledge the following people for their outstanding contributions to the Visual Prolog Computer Language and supporting Application Development Suite of Software.

### Visual Prolog - Prolog Development Center A/S Founders
Finn Grønskov (1)
Leo Schou-Jensen (1)

### Visual Prolog Project Manager
Thomas Linder Puls (1)

### Key Visual Prolog Project Staff Members
Alexander Doronin (2)
Serge Mukhin, and (2)
Carsten Kehler Holst (1)

(1) Copenhagen Denmark
(2) Saint Petersburg, Russia

And last but certainly not least, *Elizabeth Safro* from the Visual Prolog Team in the Saint Petersburg, Russia office, and *Carsten Christoffersen* from the Visual Prolog Headquarters office in Copenhagen, Denmark, for their timely and gracious support to help coordinate important issues related to this book.

My heart felt thanks go to all for bringing this fantastic and intellectually stimulating product to the international community.

CHAPTER 1

# The Prolog Language

## 1.1 How Prolog fits into Artificial Intelligence

For those who have studied other historical and conventional computer languages like maybe Basic, C, C++, Cobol, Fortran, Pascal, Forth, Ada; or, even maybe at lower levels like Assembly or even Machine Code – you know you pretty much have to hold the Computers hand through the whole program. If you give it the wrong path or data values, you will get errors. And, nothing is more frustrating than getting run-time errors with the struggle in finding where they are, particularly when the number of lines of code are huge. These are referred to as Procedural Languages; probably because under a very rigid rule of following a specific sequence of procedures, can you have any hopes in getting a program to produce the desired results. You have to be very accurate by telling the Computer exactly, line by line, what to do.

Artificial Intelligence on the other hand, has a family of languages (like Prolog, Lisp, and Scheme) which are referred to as Declarative Languages. I guess in a somewhat fuzzy way in that you 'declare' Rules for how answers are derived; and, these languages are radically different in how the code actually executes to get results or answers, as compared to their Procedural sisters. In this process of creating or writing Rules for answer derivation, you have to keep in mind you need to be prepared to deal with some amazing possibilities. For instance, maybe your Rules produce many answers – how do you capture them? What if your Rules can't find an answer, but intuitively you know answers exist. Can you guarantee your Rules won't force an endless search that produces nothing? And, with the help of interpreter versions, you can actually write Rules that write other Rules.

Here in lies the Heart of Expert Systems and the World of Artificial Intelligence.

## 1.2 Prolog Basics and General Information

Before discussing Prolog, my intent is to provide some comparison analysis with Procedural Languages you may already have familiarity with, allow you to absorb intellectually the essence of the Prolog Language, then get into Visual Prolog very specifically with useful examples. This assumes you will spend most of your time reading, studying, and getting oriented; before you actually try to write any Prolog programs. You will be encouraged to write as much as you wish when we get to Visual Prolog.

In Procedural Languages you usually begin by creating Procedures or Functions with calling Names, which are called with incoming and/or outgoing parameters. The difference being that Functions typically can have one or more incoming parameters, but only one return value or object; where as Procedures can have many incoming and outgoing parameters. Most Procedural Languages come with many built-in Procedures and Functions for tasks that are commonly called for, like reading or writing information, so you don't have to create that functionality yourself.

# THE PROLOG LANGUAGE

Procedural Language Examples:

**Procedure**
*CallingName(Parameters)*
getPartData(PartNo string, Cost real, Quantity integer)

**Function**
*CallingName(Parameters) -> Return Value/Object*
getPartPrice(PartNo string) -> Price real

In the provided example above, the naming convention used was to begin the Calling Names with a lowercase letter; and for parameters, begin Variable Names with a capital letter and Variable Types with a lowercase letter. This naming convention is quite standard in many languages, so you probably ought to keep that in mind.

Prolog on the other hand, has some similarities, but what Procedural Languages refer to as Procedures, Prolog refers to as Predicates. Predicates and their conceptual use, actually have very deep roots in the Mathematical study of Predicate Calculus. The Predicate is at heart the building blocks of the Rule(s). You use Predicates to create or write Rules to derive Truth. If the Rule contains static data only, then it is referred to as a Fact. On the other hand, if you use it with variables and implication ('if'), then it is referred to as a Rule. All Rule definitions (for Facts and Rules) take place when you provide definitions for the Predicates in a section called Clauses. Therefore, to begin writing Rules in Prolog, you must understand the two key Sections where you declare the Predicates, followed by how you define them in the Clauses. The Predicate Section lists the Predicates with their parameters (similar to Procedures); where as the Clauses Section defines the Predicates. Examples:

**Predicates**

*CallingName(parameters)*
name(Name string).
isParent(Parent string, Child string)

**Clauses**
name("Dick").     "This is a Fact"
name("Sally").    "This is a Fact"
name("John").     "This is a Fact"
name("Larry").    "This is a Fact"

isParent("John", "Sally").                              "This is a Fact"
isParent("John", "Larry").                              "This is a Fact"
isParent(P, "Dick") if name(P) and isParent(P, "Larry").   "This is a Rule"

A nice part of Prolog, after you think about it, is the language with it's Rule construction tools really consists of only 3 operators: Implication ("if"), and the logical operators of conjunction ("and") and disjunction ("or"). Most implementations of Prolog also allow some shorthand version of these operators as well like (':-' for 'if'), (',' for 'and'), and (';' for 'or'). For instance using the previous example of a Rule:

**Clauses**
isParent(P, "Dick") :- name(P), isParent(P, "Larry").

In time after you get use to it, you'll probably find very little use for the disjunction ('or') operator in Rules, because they tend to make Rules somewhat divergent as opposed to convergent. But there are some places where they can be convenient. Also, the logical Implication in Prolog is a little different than how people usually think of "if" in regular English. The Prolog use, is to say the Left Hand side of 'if' is True, <u>if and only if</u> the Right Hand side of 'if ' is True. Keep in mind you pretty much force convergences when you start tacking on conjunctions ('and') on the Right Hand side. The fewer conjunctions you provide, then maybe the more unwanted solutions you might get. Also, anything False that shows up on the Right Hand side will cause the Rule to Fail, provided you don't use disjunctions. Be very careful with the use of disjunctions, as you don't want to allow success when failure should be the proper course.

Another area in Declarative Languages (like Prolog) that differ from their Procedural sisters is their notorious uses of Lists. You will not find use of Arrays in Prolog. The older Procedural Languages were somewhat constraining in requiring fore-knowledge of space requirements for an array as well, before they could even be used; although some follow-on versions did get somewhat more flexible. Lists in Prolog are key tools for collecting data or information – both when you know ahead of time how much needs to be collected, as well as when you don't. The construction and access is based on 2 parts of the List: it's Head (the first and single element) and it's Tail (none, one, or more elements that follow). The usual written convention is [Head | Tail]. A List could be an empty List []; or, could consist of one or more elements ['a'], or [1 | 2,3,4,5]. A List could also be a List of other Lists [['a','b'],['t' |'v','x'],[],['d' |'e','f','g']]. This is an important data manipulation concept you will need to get very familiar with as you study Prolog. Another thought to keep in mind, is that although in computers there will never be any Lists with infinite elements to manipulate (they will all have a finite set of elements to deal with), in Prolog you can iteratively pick these Lists apart, one element at a time until you reach an empty List.

One more unique attribute you can tie to Prolog, which has some valuable uses; and, that is the Don't Care or Anonymous Variable parameter, written with an underscore '_'. Don't Cares are actually used when you call a Predicate and one or more of the parameters you are passing, you don't care about. It doesn't matter, because they have no Value, Logic, or Use for the current Truth you are seeking. You're probably wondering if you don't care, then why were they declared? You will understand better when you see some examples latter.

One last area I wish to discuss, before beginning some expansion, has to do with 2 tools (actually predicates themselves) within the Language of Prolog, to help manage Rule Execution. They are the Cut and Fail. Most versions of Prolog also have shorthand notation for the Cut as well ('!' the exclamation point). Their purposes are as follows:

# A GUIDE TO ARTIFICIAL INTELLIGENCE WITH VISUAL PROLOG

a. **Cut** – When you have Rules that are non-deterministic (exhibit many possible paths to a solution), there may come a time when you prefer to force it to stop looking for solutions (or, stop stacking backtrack points). That is where you place a Cut. You'll get a good understanding of some of its use, when you start getting an appreciation of Recursive Predicate Calls (this will be re-visited later).

b. **Fail** – As you learn more on how Prolog executes it search for Truth solutions, you will sometimes find it useful to prod it to search more by forcing a Failure. But keep in mind, when you first hear this you may be wondering – Oh no, am I forcing a situation where a Rule will never succeed? No, you will find with Prolog you can construct several Rules starting with a Predicate with the same Name; and, failure of one doesn't mean total failure.

As you expand your knowledge of Prolog, you will no doubt need to get beyond the basics discussed so far, so I will incrementally provide some expansion. When I discussed providing parameters for Predicates, I did it in a way you could see similarity to Procedures. There is more to understand about these Predicate declarations in the Predicates Section.

Predicate parameters must be defined in one of 2 possible ways: either use definitions that are provided by the standard or default Domain; or, you must define your own domains with declarations in a Domains Section. The Standard or Default Domain usually consists of the following entities: string, symbol, integer, real, or character. As you may have noticed, these are referred to as Type's in Procedural Languages. Most of the time, user defined domains provide a way of renaming default domain entities for uniqueness naming, isolation, and forced scoping; or, creating what are called compound domains with what is called a functor, which almost makes it look like a Function. This is also where a unique naming

## THE PROLOG LANGUAGE

convention comes into play with Prolog to identify List domains. List domains are identified using an asterisk ('*'). Examples:

**Domains**
    day    = integer.
    month = integer.
    year   = integer.
    auto   = car(string, year)    Compound Domain - car() is a Functor
    dealer = auto*                List of Autos

**Predicates**
    date(M month, D day, Y year).
    usedCarLot(dealer).

**Clauses**
    date(8, 7, 1952).
    UsedCarLot([(car("Ford", 1982), car("Volvo", 1997), car("BMW", 2005)]]).

Another issue worthy of discussion of Predicates, is that in the declaration of Predicates there also exists what are referred to as Flows for its parameters. In Prolog and the art of writing Rules, you have the muscle of writing Rules in such a manner that the parameters can be incoming or outgoing or both, and the program under execution and its search for Truth, will experiment with all possible options based on the provided Rules and Facts. As you get use to it though, you might find it worthwhile to define the flows yourself for maybe some complex Rules; or there may be times when you want to force the program to use your defined flows. Another example ('o' for Output 'i' for Input):

**Predicates**
    date(M month, D day, Y year) **(i, i, i) (o, o, o)**

Last, in regard to Predicates, I will mention that Prolog allows you to contend with the possibility that the search should result in a single solution (deterministic) or there may be many possible solutions (non-deterministic). As you start using varying Rules (deterministic

◄ A GUIDE TO ARTIFICIAL INTELLIGENCE WITH VISUAL PROLOG

as well as non-deterministic), you will sometimes find conveniences in your program designs to identify their purposes ahead of time, as well as find useful discovery with compiler generated errors when not considered. These can also be defined in the Predicates section, but some compilers will keep you honest when they find fallacies. Declaration example:

**Predicates**
date(M month, D day, Y year) **determ** (i, i, i) (o, o, o)

This should be enough for now considering Predicate declarations, but I will need to expand more when we get to Visual Prolog specifically.

So far you should now be familiar with 3 sections used with Prolog: Domains, Predicates, and Clauses. I will briefly cover two more: Constants and Database.

Constants are fairly simple and similar to how they are dealt with in Procedural Languages. Typically you would provide these definitions right after you identify your domains, but they can precede domains too.

The Database section on the other hand, is quite unique with Prolog in that when Prolog was first started, this was how long term information was dealt with for query as well as manipulation, which became the heart of what was fascinatingly termed 'Consulting' – kind of like consulting the Expert. The Database section also usually precedes the Predicate section. Keep in mind, pretty much in all languages; you typically can't use something until it has already been declared. You can also uniquely name Database sections to keep them separate, save them separately, as well as consult them individually. Partial Example (Complete with 5 sections, but code is incomplete):

# THE PROLOG LANGUAGE

**Domains**
```
iron      = string
irons     = iron*
wood      = string
woods     = wood*
driver    = string
putter    = string
golfClubs = bag(irons, woods, driver, putter)
score     = integers*
```

**Constants**
```
par = 72
```

**Database - golfPlayers**
player(Name string, Clubs golfClubs, Age integer, Sex symbol, Handicap real)

**Predicates**
```
playerScore(P player, S score).
addScore( T integer, S score).
getScore(S integer).
```

**Clauses**
getScore(S) :- playerScore(_, Slist), addScore(S, Slist).

addScore(_,[]).
addScore(S, [H | T]):-
    addScore(Snew, T),
    S = Snew + H.

To finish the intellectual discussion of Prolog, so we can get more quickly to Visual Prolog, I need to explain a little about how Prolog programs execute. Most versions of Prolog usually give you two ways to start your Prolog programs: one way is to use a Prolog Interpreter which you just start feeding it predicates you have already defined; and, the other way is to create what is called a Goal section where you identify which Predicate or Rule to use to start your program. When you get into Visual Prolog, these are accommodated by the Prolog Inference Engine (PIE) sample application that comes with it; or, it creates the Goal section for you when you create an Application yourself respectively. I'll explain more when we get to Visual Prolog.

At any rate once Prolog starts, when it finds a Predicate that has been defined by the same name more than once, it goes to the first one and sets a Backtrack Point, so that if there is failure, it will come back and proceed to the next one. Please keep in mind that as you start writing complex Rules, with predicates that call other predicates, and with conjunctive connections through implication; several complex Backtrack points can get set. So you will need to prepare yourself to a slightly different mind set when you approach diagnostic analysis of program control, as Prolog is quite different from its Procedural sisters. During execution when a rule succeeds, Prolog will stop looking for truth with that Rule and assume it has what you wanted. If there are other possibilities you want it to look for using that Rule, then this is where you may need to force failure; however, doing so, you need to have a Rule in the set that will lead to success, so the program continues as desired. Again, this is where use of the Cut and Fail predicates may provide some usefulness in the desire for program efficiency.

## 1.3 Summary

The Prolog Sections within a program

Domains
Constants
Database
Predicates
Goal
Clauses

Prolog Operators

Implication    if     :-
Conjunction    and    ,
Disjunction    or     ;

**Note:** *Actually there is a 4th (unary) logic operator called 'not',*

## THE PROLOG LANGUAGE

*which can be valuable in the search for truth, when some of the known facts (or derived facts through implications) are known not to be true. However, Visual Prolog treats it as a predicate 'not()', as opposed to an operator. See 'not' in Built-in entities of the Language Reference Wiki.*

### Special Predicates

Cut !
Fail

### Unique Prolog Variables

List         [Head | Tail]
Anonymous    _

### Prolog Predicate declaration attributes

callingName     autoDealer()
parameters      Variable and Domain
determinism     determ or nondeterm
Flow Patterns   (i, i) (i, o) (o, i) (o, o)

**Note:** *For more intellectual reading about Prolog historical development, search for 'Horn Clauses' discussion, which is what Prolog was built on. I'm sure much can be found on the internet; however, Eduardo Costa in his 'Visual Prolog for Tyros' as well as Thomas de Boar in his 'Beginners' Guide to Visual Prolog' provides an excellent discussion as well. You can find these at the Visual Prolog Web Site.*

CHAPTER 2

# Visual Prolog

## 2.1 For Beginners

### 2.1.1 How to Download and Install

It is assumed you are using a Microsoft Windows platform and are interested in downloading Visual Prolog. Please keep in mind if you are using a version of the Microsoft Operating System that Microsoft does not support anymore, maybe Visual Prolog is not for you. Visual Prolog also is not for UNIX or Apple/Macintosh audiences either – at this current time.

If you don't know where to find it and have access to the Internet with a Browser, then go to http://www.visual-prolog.com/ and select the 'Download' Tab option from the Initial screen. On the Download screen, you can either select the Personal Version (which is free), or select the Commercial Version (which is not free). If you want the 'Commercial Version' you can either use a credit card to make your purchase; or, follow their directions to make your purchase without a credit card.

The information provided on their web site is quite strait forward with instructions on how to download. The file they use currently to download the Personal Version is about 20M in size, so keep that in mind for bandwidth requirements depending on what you are using to move information on the internet: 56K modem, DSL, etc.

Once downloaded, you will be provided instructions on installation. I think the important thing to remember is where you placed it on your system when it was downloaded. I maintain specific locations on my system for information that I download off the Internet. That way I know where to find them if I encounter some kind of problem later on - like the need to re-install and avoid the need to reconnection to the internet to download it again. The file you receive should look similar to 'vip7201pe.msi'. I think the naming convention reflects Visual Prolog version 7.2, maybe Release 1, Personal Edition; and, uses a Microsoft Software Installation interface. Because Visual Prolog evolves over time, the version you get may differ from the name I provided.

After you have downloaded Visual Prolog and Installed it, go ahead and start it up so you can polish or finish some other installation niceties. First, make sure you are still connected to the internet and find the Menu option under 'Web' to check for updates. This is nice to do occasionally as well, because you will want to keep your version of Visual Prolog up to date as enhancing developments get released. Next, go to the Menu option under 'Help' and install the examples. You will no doubt be exploring many of these as you get familiar with Visual Prolog and expand both your knowledge and experience. Keep in mind the PDC also sometime updates these examples too, as well as provide others that are not packaged with the product, which you will need to periodically look for on their web site.

Now that you have it installed, it will help to properly orient you so you know how and where to look for Help or Assistance when you get snagged or need information.

## 2.1.2 Orientation – How and where to look for Help

Visual Prolog happens to be very rich in information sources with a tremendous wealth of information available in several forms both packaged with Visual Prolog, as well as on-line through the internet to their web links.

The hard part may be which ones do you use and when? In the References Chapter of this Book I list the following references:

    4.1 Built in Predicates
    4.2 Program Foundation Class (PFC)
    4.3 Help Avenues
        4.3.1 Built in Help
        4.3.2 PDC Resources on the Web
            4.3.2.1 Language Reference Wiki
            4.3.2.2 Knowledge Base
            4.3.2.3 Tutorials
            4.3.2.4 Discussion Forum

I will provide a lot more detail about these references in the Reference Chapter of this Book, but the reason why I list them now is to help orient you. The Visual Prolog IDE Menu also can provide great links to the assorted help features available, to include access to their web site. See the IDE menu items below.

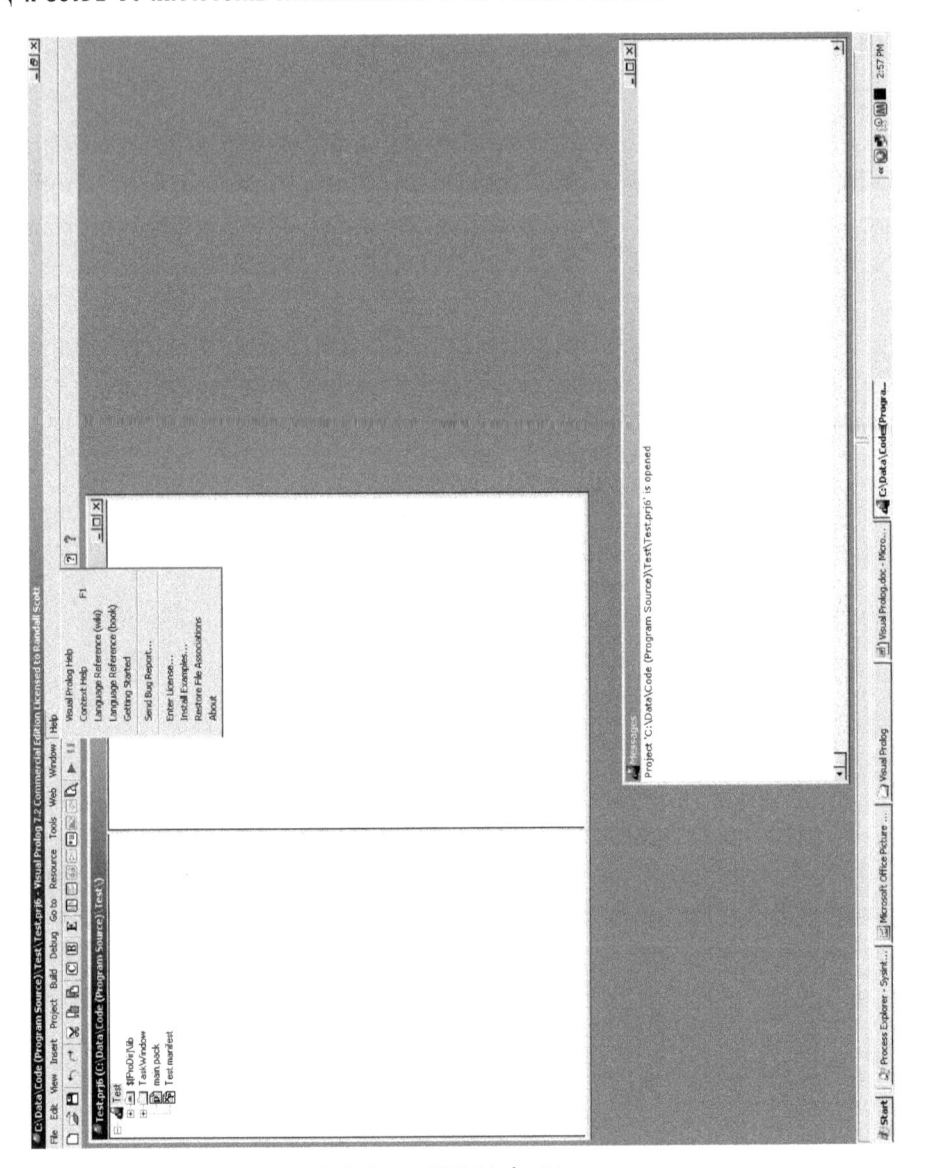

2.1.2.a - IDE Help Menu

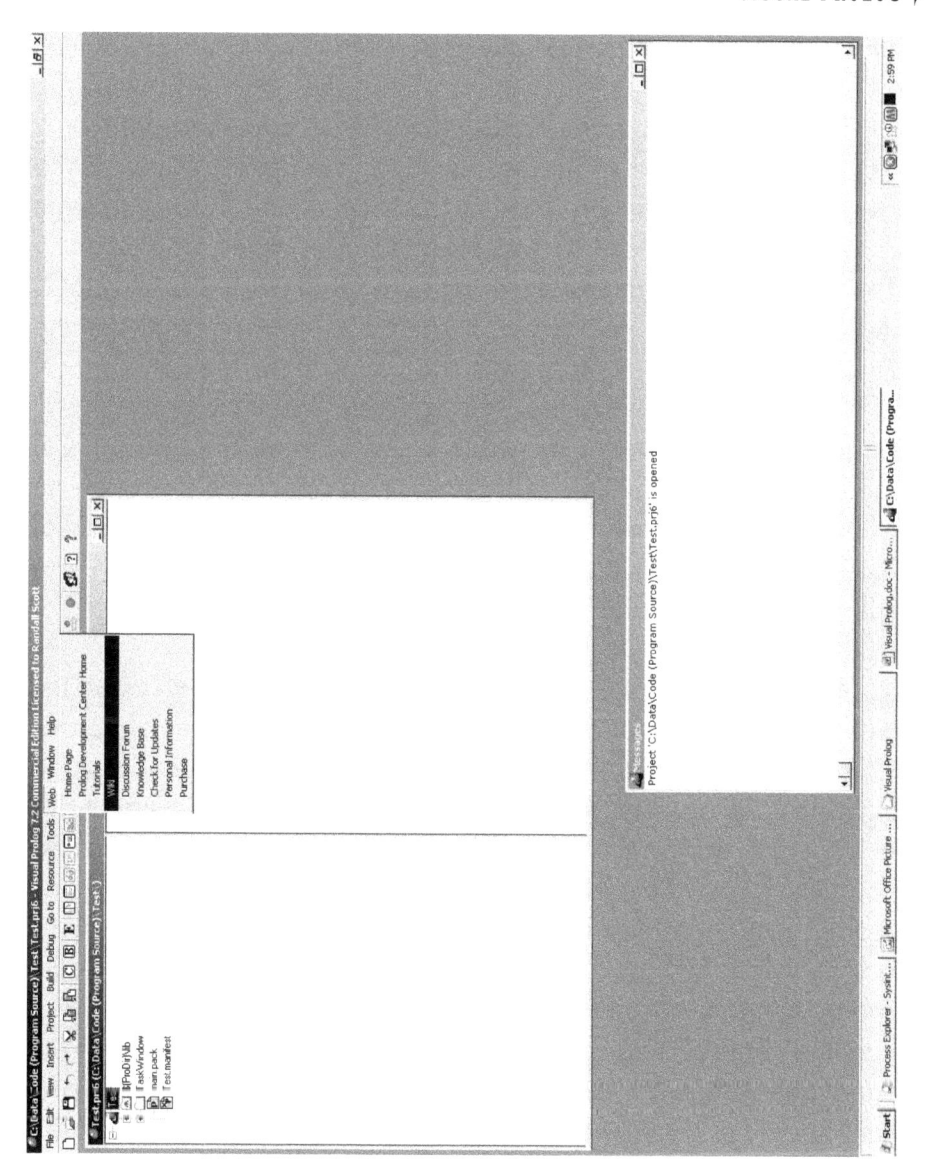

2.1.2.b - IDE Web Help Menu

Visual Prolog comes with many Built-in Predicates, which as I mentioned earlier for Procedural Languages, these help eliminate the need to write the common functionality yourself. Some are historical, but you will need to become familiar with what already exists and what they are typically used for.

The Program Foundation Class (PFC) is also important in 2 ways. First, it is used somewhat similar to the Built-in Predicates to help provide functionality that you can use without having to write it yourself, with a focus on typical application development issues. The other handy truth to keep in mind, is that knowledge of what is in the PFC can also help you distinguish the difference between the Personal Version as compared to the Commercial Version. The list of PFC resources listed in the Help option to Visual Prolog Help, will list all the PFC resources available in the Commercial Version. On the other hand, when you start creating an application or open an example with the Personal Version, look at the Explorer like Visual Prolog Project Tree under App\$(ProDir)\pfc. This PFC listing is a subset of the other and nothing can get added to it.

As for the Help Avenues listed for both Built-in as well as on the web through PDC, I'll save most of the discussion for the References Chapter. However, I think I need to expand one issue though right now because of its importance, it's difficultly to research for newcomers, and very critical to help understand an often reported compiler error when you are new to creating Predicates in Visual Prolog. I also promised earlier that I would expand more when I got to Visual Prolog. This is what is referred to as the Predicate Mode when you declare Predicates in the Predicates Section. You can find very good discussion of Predicate Modes in the on-line Wiki Language Reference or the Language Reference Book packaged with Visual Prolog; however, you will not find it under the discussion of Predicates. It's actually located in the discussion of Domains, as Visual Prolog also defines what Predicate Domains are. Previously I only provided 2 of these which were actually the only 2 when Prolog first started: determ and nondeterm. Visual Prolog actually currently provides six Predicate Modes: erroneous, failure, procedure, determ, multi, and nondeterm. All of these are based on whether or not they involve Success, Failure, Setting Backtrack Points, or Nothing. I'll restate what the Language Reference says about them: "Predicate modes can be described by the following sets:

```
erroneous = {}
failure = {Fail}
procedure = {Succeed}
determ = {Fail, Succeed}
multi = {Succeed, BacktrackPoint}
nondeterm = {Fail, Succeed, BacktrackPoint}"
```

The important issue regarding Predicate declarations that I want you to understand is that Visual Prolog uses default settings if you don't specifically provide them yourself. Most of the time this is quite handy; however, you must understand what Visual Prolog assigns for you if you do not assign them yourself. I'll use an example to explain some of the defaults Visual Prolog will assign. Example:

**Predicates**
   isFather(Father string, Child string)

Visual Prolog will assign Predicate Mode of 'procedure' and a Flow of (i,i).

As you can see, 'procedure' Mode only involves success which might not be what you're interested in, or what your 'Rule' may try to do. Also, Mode nesting can get quite complicated particularly if they get mixed.

As a final comment, initially I recommend using Visual Prolog Help for most of your research on the Visual Prolog language and application development assistance. The Language Reference Book is great; but, may be a little difficult to read. You can also go to the Web Forum and search for information as well. In addition, when you register your product you can join the Forum and post questions of your own.

### 2.1.3 Tutorials

Visual Prolog has several Tutorial references you can use to learn Visual Prolog. They are not packaged with the product; although several examples do come with the product that is useful to learn Visual Prolog as well.

Their web site has a special Tutorial page you can go to and download several different flavors of tutorials. Some are titled Fundamentals: (Basic), GUI, the Business Logical Layer, and the Data Layer. There is one for Environment Overview. And, there also currently exists an Index on the Web page, with many examples that explain a good portion of the functionality built into the PFC family. Unfortunately, some of these examples only refer to and are applicable to the Commercial Version.

Most important though are two teaching tools mentioned before: one titled 'Visual Prolog for Tyros' and the other 'A Beginners' Guide to Visual Prolog'. I recommend starting with the one titled 'A Beginners' Guide to Visual Prolog'. It would be nice if it were available as a paper book, as it contains more than 200 pages of really great tutorial information.

### 2.1.4 The Prolog Inference Engine (PIE)

When we were in the Microsoft DOS world, programming was a little easier in that you didn't have any Graphical User Interfaces (GUIs) to deal with, or Event Handling, or anything close to Object Oriented Programming with Instance Management and Polymorphism. For beginners, that is quite a bit to chew on.

So if you are a beginner, I highly recommend you start with the Prolog Inference Engine (PIE) that comes with Visual Prolog as an example. You'll need to compile it before running it, but it is not very hard. The 'A Beginners' Guide to Visual Prolog' provides some real good instructions as well as starter examples. The reason

## VISUAL PROLOG

I recommend PIE, is that although it will somewhat resemble a GUI anyway, it provides a DOS like window to interactively provide commands (Predicates) to a Prolog Interpreter. This will be very valuable for you to watch and learn Prolog Rule construction, execution, as well as see the answers derived.

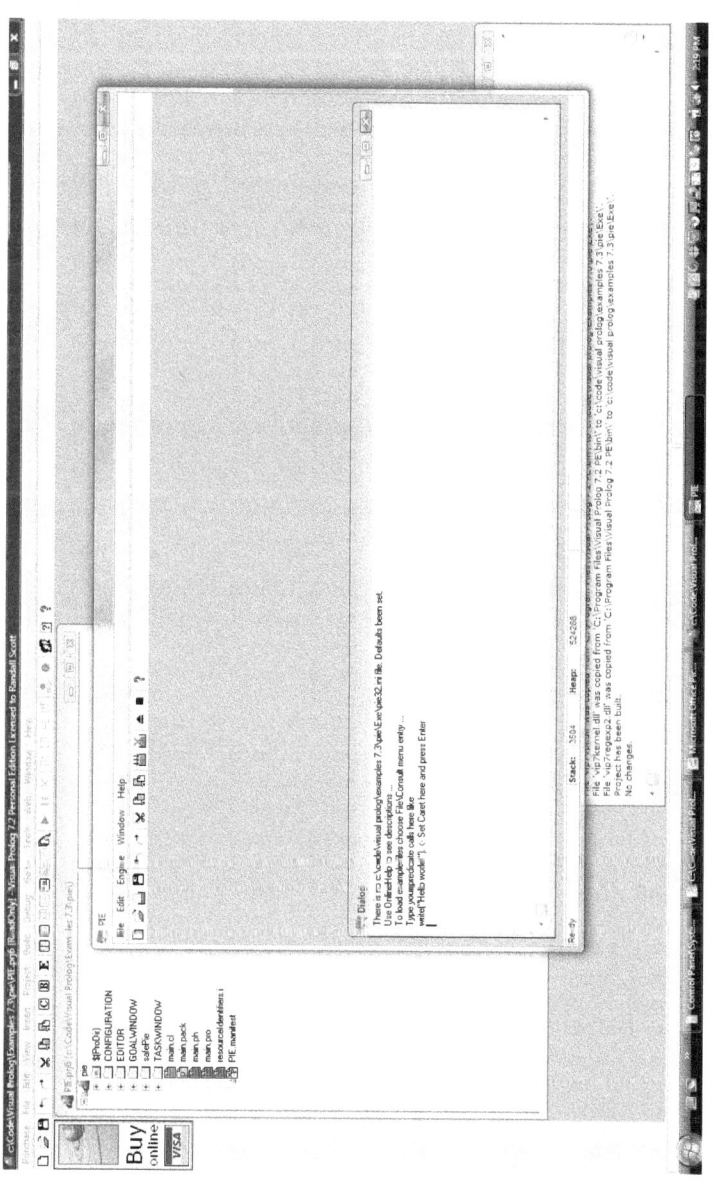

2.1.4 - PIE

After you get use to it, you will know how to create and save these programs for later recall, so you don't have to type them in again; or, modify for a slightly different concept you are trying to explore. Keep in mind though, PIE is a really great and simple tool to teach and learn Prolog Rules which premiers Inference and Truth Derivation; however, it is not a tool for complex Applications.

## 2.2 Past the Beginner Mode

Considering the tutorial references and guides I have already listed, I see no need in repeating what has already been said, or can be referred to, unless I find issues worthy of repeating. I, on the other hand, plan to try and articulated important concepts using a different presentation method or style.

I think most previous provided Visual Prolog teaching references usually begin by getting the User to create objects (like a Form, a Toolbar, or a Menu), then take you immediately to the Code Expert, and start dealing with the Event Handlers. In a slightly different approach, I want to highlight and emphasize the excellent modularity features that Visual Prolog provides; and, in the Sample Application Section demonstrate these features as an Application is developed.

To begin with, it is very important to understand Scoping and how Visual Prolog accommodates it.

### 2.2.1 Scoping

Scoping is an important Software Engineering concept in several aspects of writing computer programs, no matter which language is used. To begin with, when writing code some parts of it may be desirable to be Private (where only a program module or a portion of it has access), as opposed to Public (which may be accessible from anywhere in the program). In the old days, lack of Scoping was the driving forces to help get rid of dangerous Global Variables

## VISUAL PROLOG

and the infamous GOTO statements. However, it can sometimes be a 2 edged sword creating both conveniences as well as inconveniences.

A large benefit of good Scoping has been the ability to more easily write very large Application Programs, with many programmers, which incorporate the extremely valuable Software Engineering attributes of Maximum Cohesion with Minimum Coupling. Another benefit has been much better compiler designs that lead to more reliable code with almost zero free run-time errors.

Visual Prolog has been designed to accommodate Scoping in several areas. Of the 2 more important ones; one is related to Object Oriented Programming compatibility paradigms, where as the other one embraces Programmer oriented code development and management features. This can be of great importance as the program grows in size and when many programmers are involved. How do you organize very important pieces and parts for both programmers as well as compilers? I'll concentrate on the second for now.

As you get more familiar with Visual Prolog, you will notice some file naming conventions that are used that contribute to scoping. Being somewhat similar to the Packaging concept embraced in the very early beginning of the Ada Language in the 1980's, Visual Prolog has been designed to help separate the Declarations from the Specification or Implementation – in a similar way as to what leads to what is visible vs. what is hidden. The Visual Prolog basic unit is a Package and has the '.pack' filename extension. Within the Package, you may create and organize classes (with separate files for declarations vs. implementations), interfaces, as well as modules.

There are also a few other programming concepts where separate files are used to isolate concepts and help ease code management for the Programmer, as well as the Compiler. I'll list the file name extensions used for these concepts:

**Compiler Generated (User Modified) and Managed Program Source Files**
Package .pack
Package Header .ph

**IDE and User Written and Managed Program Source Files**
Class Declaration .cl
Class Implementation .pro
Interface .i

*Note: Classes are usually used in the Object Oriented world to create Objects under program control during execution. If a Programmer defined Class does not create Objects, then it is considered a Module.*

**Resource Descriptions and Application Development** Support Files
window .win
bitmap .bmp
dialog .dlg
menu .mnu
toolbar .tb
icon .ico
form .frm
cursor .cur

## 2.2.2 Database Environment

In Visual Prolog, there are actually two different Database environments available: the Traditional Database which has a separate Section for declarations in your source code (as mentioned earlier); and, one that provides a means for managing huge Databases with built-in sorting features. The Traditional Database is available for everyone, as it is in both the Personal and Commercial Versions; and, the one I will be focusing on for now. The other one is only available with the Commercial Version: see ChainDB under the PFC in Visual Prolog Help for more information about a Prolog managed external Database; and, ODBC for connections to other external Databases.

Although the Traditional Database is somewhat lacking in providing built-in sorting features for database information (there is none), it is still quite a handy resource to use. You will need to get familiar with the following built-in Predicates which will be used a lot with Traditional Databases:

assert
asserta
assertz
retract
retractall
findall

Use of the **assert**, **asserta**, and **assertz** Predicates help you put data into the database. **assert** and **asserta** are the same - **asserta** was created afterword's to give a more obvious place as to where you want to insert information into your database (at the beginning); where as **assertz** places information on the end of the database. Keep in mind this does not sort your database, but knowing Database entries are very similar to Predicates, Prolog will always start looking at the beginning. On the other hand, **retract** is used to remove individual database entries, and **retractall** can remove all database entries. Lastly, **findall** is very useful as a single predicate to collect everything you're interested in, into a List for further processing. The **findall** Predicate is quite useful (more than just internal databases), although it can sometimes be difficult when the data you want to capture are defined with complex functors.

Here is an excellent time and place in emphasizing the importance of getting use to List Variables and useful Prolog Predicates for manipulating List information. The PFC provides most of the List manipulation Predicates needed, so you don't have to write them yourself; however, I recommend you explore how these List Manipulation Predicates work (through PIE) and maybe create a few of your own, as these are truly one of the large muscles used by Prolog to help with Truth Derivation. You'll also get an appreciation for use of the Lists, Anonymous Variables, and Recursion.

### 2.2.3 The Integrated Development Environment

The Visual Prolog Integrated Development Environment (IDE) is a very powerful tool; and, certainly eases the process of developing applications. It contains a very busy set of windows to get use to; however, as you get use to it you will be marveled at how powerful it truly is. One of my favorite portions are the windows available to help debug a program, which show the Run Stack, Variables for current Clause, Facts, Threads, and Modules. Probably the only real hard part is figuring how to properly set Break Points, sometimes due to programs that exhibit complex Backtracking.

I will not try to teach you how to get around in the Integrated Development Environment, as plenty of resources are already at your disposal for use. The built-in Visual Prolog Help provides an excellent specific section oriented to the IDE. Also, you will find great help by reading the 'Beginners' Guide to Visual Prolog' and 'Visual Prolog for Tyros', which in addition provide examples for you to get hands-on familiarity.

### 2.2.4 Application Development

When you have reached confidence for use of Prolog to Derive Truth using implication, conjunctions, and disjunctions (at least minimally with Predicates and Clauses through PIE), then you are ready to explore Application Development.

Applications will need to make Prolog look mostly transparent with Windows which incorporate Dialog Boxes, Menus, and Toolbars for instance. Visual Prolog provides tremendous features that help create the windowing features like Windows, Dialog Boxes, Forms, Menus, and Toolbars; however, it is limited in that after these objects are created it does not know what you want them to do or provide. This is where Visual Prolog provides some nice interfacing tools to deal with some of the IDE created features like Menus; however, other parts must be dealt with entry into the Code Expert where you will need to write Prolog Source code - in essence modifying some already provided source code. A somewhat misleading feature of Visual Prolog is that some places will take you into the Code Expert of Program Source files which you might not be aware of. That is why I recommend getting very familiar with the filename extensions used, as you can enter these files yourself just as the Code Expert does and you know where and why you are there. If you are a beginner, the Code Expert can be somewhat intimidating in the fear of changing or deleting something that may cause the whole program to bomb – which if you are not careful, this can happen.

If you use some of the provided Tutorials which take you to the Code Expert, they often provide examples which you can easily copy and paste. However, the copy and paste operation isn't really teaching you completely in what you need to know to write your own source code. It is helpful though in seeing examples that work. This is where I emphasis the importance of understanding Predicate declaration information and what the default Predicate settings are. The better you understand Predicate Declaration information, the better you will understand how they are defined in all the Clause Sections.

At this point I will leave the discussion of Application Development for later on, when I will use a sample Application to discuss other important Application Development issues.

### 2.2.5 Other useful Commercial Application Features

For Applications that provide potential marketable features, you may wish to explore procuring the Commercial Version of Visual Prolog. These obviously are features that explain and clarify providing a version of Visual Prolog worthy of learning Prolog, as well as minimal application development for FREE through the Personal Edition Version, as opposed to the more feature rich Commercial Version.

For example, maybe you would like for your application to be able to connect to other nice Database Systems like Oracle, or SQL Server, or Access, or MySQL using ODBC tools – or, use the nice Visual Prolog Database System with the B+ Trees under ChainDB. Maybe you would like for your application to automatically send email using the Simple Mail Transport Protocol (SMTP). Maybe you would like to use Visual Prolog to develop Web Applications for the internet. There are many more nice features available with the Commercial Version of the product with many more currently under development.

With reference to the Visual Prolog web site, you will see other significant differences between the 2 versions as well (Personal vs. Commercial), and have a good idea of what is available only with the Commercial Version. Although the Commercial Version is not Free, it is quite fairly priced.

## 2.2.6 Prolog Classic Examples

Among many possible program examples, it is only fitting to provide (or maybe repeat), what may be considered Classic Programs for Prolog. With these examples you should also get an appreciation for use of Lists, the Anonymous Variable, as well as Recursion.

1. List Manipulation Predicates

**Member:** See if item is in the List
*Note: This only works for symbols, however, you could provide a large list with an answer showing all the members, as opposed to verifying just one. This is also a good example of Tail Recursion in that the member() Predicate calls itself as the last step in the second clause definition for member().*

```
domains
   name     = symbol
   namelist = name*
```

## VISUAL PROLOG

**predicates**
member(name, namelist)

**clauses**
member(Name, [Name|_]).
member(Name, [_|Tail]) if member(Name, Tail).

Try:   1. member(tom, [ann | dick, jane, sally, tom, zack]).
       2. member(X, [ann | dick, jane, sally, tom, zack]).

**Append:** Add an item to a List
*Note: This only works for integers; however, you will find it fascinating on how you can call it and mix the Flow patterns: add one item to a list, combine 2 lists, or see how a list can be split.*

**domains**
integerlist = integer*

**predicates**
append(integerlist, integerlist, integerlist)

**clauses**
append([], List, List).
append([X | L1], List2, [X | L3]) if append(L1, List2, L3).

Try: 1. append([1, 2, 3], [5, 6], L).
     2. append([1, 2], [3], L) and append(L, L, LL).

**Length:** Find the length of a List
*Note: Again this only works with integers. This happens to be a very handy routine to see how large a List really is. This routine also provides an example of recursion, but not specifically Tail Recursion.*

**domains**
list = integer*

**predicates**
length_of(list, integer)

**clauses**
length_of([], 0).
length_of([_ | T], L) if length_of(T, TailLength) and L = TailLength + 1.

Try: length_of([1, 2, 3, 4, 5, 6], L).

# A GUIDE TO ARTIFICIAL INTELLIGENCE WITH VISUAL PROLOG

**Sort**: Sort a List
*Note: Sorting Lists are usually done in one of 3 ways: Exchange Sort, Insertion Sort, and Selection Sort. Since Insertion Sort is somewhat easy, I'll provide an example of it.*

```
domains
    number = integer
    list    = number*

predicates
    insertion_sort(list, list)
    insert(number, list, list)
    asc_order(number, number)

clauses
    insertion_sort([], []).
    insertion_sort([X | Tail], Sorted_List) if
        insertion_sort(Tail, Sorted_Tail) and insert(X, Sorted_Tail,
            Sorted_List).

    insert(X, [Y | Sorted_List], [Y | Sorted_List1]) if
        asc_order(X,Y) and Cut and insert(X, Sorted_List, Sorted_List1).
    insert(X, Sorted_List, [X | Sorted_List]).

    asc_order(X, Y) if X > Y.
```

Try: 1. insertion_sort([4, 7, 3, 9], S).
     2. insertion_sort([7, 6, 5, 4, 3, 2, 1], S).

2. Predicate Recursion for an Arithmetic problem.

**Factorial**: The mathematical Factorial of a given number.
*Note: This is another example of regular Recursion as opposed to Tail Recursion to get the factorial value of a given Integer. The example also uses Real numbers to accommodate the limitation of binary represented for very large Integers.*

```
predicates
    factorial(integer, real)

clauses
    factorial(1, 1) if Cut.
    factorial(X, FactX) if
        Y = X -1 and
```

# VISUAL PROLOG

>factorial(Y, FactY) and
>FactX = X * FactY.
Try: 1. factorial(25, X).
>2. factorial(31342, X).

3. Forced Backtracking to get all Answers

**Output**: An example which is not unique, but provides insight.
*Note: This example was chosen for its simplicity to demonstrate a technique to force Prolog to get all the answers and not stop with success on the first one. The fail will cause Prolog to Backtrack to country() and try again. When it runs out of countries, the first print_countries clause fails and the second one is called which always succeeds.*

>**predicates**
>country(symbol)
>print_countries
>
>**clauses**
>country(england).
>country(france).
>country(germany).
>country(denmark).
>
>print_countries if
>country(X) and
>write(X) and
>nl and              newline command
>fail.
>
>print_countries.

4. Transitivity and Inheritance Inferences

>**Transitivity Inference**: Mathematically if X=Y, and Y=Z, then X=Z.
>*Note: Below, a() defines a relationship.*
>
>In Prolog:    a(X,Y) if a(X,Z) and a(Z,Y).
>
>**Inheritance Inference**: A single fact that may apply to many.
>*Note: Below, b() inherits with respect to relationship predicate c().*
>
>In Prolog:    b(X, Value) if c(X, Y) and b(Y, Value).

# ◂ A GUIDE TO ARTIFICIAL INTELLIGENCE WITH VISUAL PROLOG

b(X, Value) if c(Y, X) and b(Y, Value).

5. Collect Data into a List

**findall Predicate**: For most Prologs, this is a built-in Predicate.
*Note: A nice simple predicate to collect information into a single List.*

**domains**
  name   = string
  points = real
  list   = points*

**predicates**
  baseball(name, points)
  sum_list(list, points, integer)
  report_average_score

**clauses**
  basketball("Ohio State", 88.0).
  basketball("Michigan", 73.0).
  basketball("Michigan State", 65.0).
  basketball("Purdue", 92.0).
  baseketall("UCLA", 81.0).

  report_average_score if
    findall(Points, basketball(_, Points), Point_List) and
    sum_list(Point_List, Sum, Number) and
    Average = Sum / Number and
    write("Average Points = ", Average).

  sum_list([], 0, 0).
  sum_list([H|T], Sum, Number) if
    sum_list(T, Sum1, Number1) and
    Sum = H + Sum1 and
    Number = Number1 + 1.

# CHAPTER 3

# Sample Application

## 3.1 Application Discussion

I think at this point it would be good to walk you through a sample Application. To begin with, you don't just come up with an idea of what you want to explore with an application, then jump on a computer and start slinging code. There is a systemic process you need to develop when traversing the process of Application development. This systematic process can be used with any Computer Language and most times will differ slightly with each individual; however, the major concepts are virtually universal.

Begin, if you will, by putting your idea on paper. Kind of like an outline for a research project you are exploring to produce a Thesis on. This is where your Application Design Considerations take place.

## 3.2 Application Design Considerations

While studying and formulating strategy for your application, you need a starting point. Most applications involve collecting and manipulating User provided information, so consider the User information for a while.

Good questions to ask are:

- What will you expect them to provide?
- How should you translate that information for the Computer to deal with; like symbols vs. strings; or, integers vs. real?
- How do you want to interact with the Users?
- Most likely you will have them interact through a Window, but what other aspects need to be considered; for example like Menus, Toolbars, Dialog Boxes, or Message Boxes?
- Will you need to deal with large quantities of Data which may require sorting?
- Will you need to consider external storage for involved data?

Some other aspects to consider are:

- Is this an application well suited for Artificial Intelligence; or, would it be more easily dealt with using a Procedural Language?
    o Will the program be used to search for some form of Truth?
    o Can Implication be useful in finding solutions?
    o Are some of the application problems oriented toward the possibility of multiple solutions?
- How simple can you make the User interfaces? The simpler the better.
- What is the typical education level of the projected User community?

This part of the process is really still a rough sketch of the desired outcome; however if well organized, it should put you in a good position to start partitioning your application for Incremental Programming.

## 3.3 Incremental Programming

Incremental Programming is an important concept to acquire with skill. It allows you to gradually piece your application together, while focusing on assorted program aspects that sometimes get over looked. Troubling program aspects that if not dealt with early on, then when the application becomes huge, they are almost impossible to locate and correct. Can your program accommodate every possible User action? Hopefully the program accommodates at least all the common ones. Can you properly deal with User errors? Can you set your program up in a manner that avoids User Errors?

When you start creating an application in Visual Prolog, it already starts out with significant portions of the Source code built for you. This is convenient in that you are freed from having to produce it yourself; however, you need to develop a comfort zone with what Visual Prolog provides for you, so you can more easily modify the sections required with the Code Expert. The Sample Application that I will be exploring takes a slightly different approach, in that you will be initially minimally dealing with what Visual Prolog provides, and focusing more on your own Source Code to gain a good appreciation of modularity and scoping. This will also make it somewhat easier to demonstrate the concept of Incremental Programming.

### 3.3.1 Starting Data

Usually all Applications will manipulate some form of Data, maybe to collect it, extract certain meaningful entities, and output desired results. Most often Applications are designed to interact with Users; although there are others which minimally involve human Users, and focus on some form of machinery and environmental conditions.

So, now is a good time to discuss a specific Application as well as address the subjects of Design Considerations, Incremental Programming, and Starting Data. The Application I will explore, is to provide some meaning for numbers to pick for a lottery. The lottery I will be using is the Mega Millions from the state of Georgia. What is nice about this lottery is that they have a web site that will allow you to download the entire history of all numbers called since its inception.

You can currently find this web site at: www.galottery.com/stc/home/index.jsp. This will take you right to the page with the download data of interest; however, you can also just go to www.galottery.com and search. I hope the web address doesn't change in the near future; however, if it does I think you'll still benefit and maybe even find parallel applicability to other data collection applications.

For Design Considerations, Incremental Programming, and Starting Data - I will want to start by download the lottery history for the Georgia Mega Millions Lotto, and format the information so it can be imported into my Visual Prolog program. Once Imported, I would like to analyze the data to find interesting aspects of numbers already called. Knowing that for each Mega Millions Lotto there are 5 Regular Ball numbers called as well as one Money Ball number called with different pay off significance for both categories of numbers; and, depending on which ones were selected. Some good questions to explore for both categories are:

    a. Are there any numbers that have never been called?
    b. Which are the 10 least called numbers?
    c. Which are the 10 most called numbers?
    d. Which are the 10 oldest numbers called?

To help avoid User error, I plan to avoid having the user type any information into the program. Instead, the User interaction will be limited to menu selections and buttons. Probably the hardest User interaction part is to get them to correctly format the downloaded

## SAMPLE APPLICATION

Lotto information so there are no problems with importing it. Once imported under a Menu provided option, the program will acquire the historical information to answer the questions asked above. This historical information will be saved so it can be reused as often as desired until it becomes necessary to download updated Historical Information.

The program will also provide options under Menu control to get numbers. This could be designed to just randomly select numbers irrespective of the historical information; or, solely based on the historical information; or, in combination with the historical information collected. Incrementally, we will start with the data import portion, followed by answering the questions for the historical information, then working to acquire the combination of random numbers, then (in conjunction with the previous activities) how to display or output the desired information, and lastly a means of providing useful User Help.

Some things to think about with regard to this application, is there are no guarantees any program can provide you with the winning numbers for a truly random Lottery. However, even though you may not be able to select all the winning numbers of a lottery, you can logically pick numbers that may contribute more consistently to smaller prizes. At any rate, I think this Lottery Application is a great tool for learning Artificial Intellegence with Visual Prolog.

### 3.3.2 Data Importing

The first part of this application will be to manually download the Mega Lotto History Data. You can currently get the data at http://www.galottery.com/stc/games/megaMillions.jsp#results. Make sure you select the "Download ALL results from game inception". Also, make sure you provide a good location on your computer as to where it gets saved. You should get a file under the name of "MegaMillionsHistory.csv" which is related to Microsoft Excel

Comma Separated Values.

When you open the file with Microsoft Excel, you will find over 700 sets of numbers called so far. In order to prepare it for import into the Visual Prolog Application we will be creating, we will clean it slightly and convert it to a Text File under the name of "Stats.txt". To do this, open it in Microsoft Excel (or whatever Spreadsheet application you use) and delete all rows previous to the number sets; then use 'Save As' to save it with the name of 'Stats' with a file type of '.txt'. Now you could open the 'Stats.txt' with Microsoft Notepad, which will be handy later on; but, there are a few more modifications we need to do that can not be done with Notepad.

Therefore the next step is to open the 'Stats.txt' file with Microsoft Word (or whatever Word Processing application you use) and select the Edit/Replace option to make the following additional modifications:

    a. With non-printable characters displayed, replace all Tabs with a Space character.
    b. Replace all slashes ('/') with a space character.
    c. Replace all 'space MB=' with nothing.
    d. Replace all Hyphens with a space character.

**Before Change**
3/31/2009 tab 14-39-47-48-53 space space MB=29
3/27/2009 tab 10-15-24-38-50 space space MB=19
3/24/2009 tab 04-25-34-43-44 space space MB=45
.
.
.

**After Change**
3 31 2009 14 39 47 48 53 29
3 27 2009 10 15 24 38 50 19
3 24 2009 04 25 34 43 44 45
.
.
.

# SAMPLE APPLICATION

Make sure there is nothing before the number sets or after the number sets. The goal is to provide the Visual Prolog program with generic 9 Terms per line for each Mega Millions Lotto number set. For program control the meaning will be: the first 3 terms are the Date, the next 5 are the Regular Numbers Called, and the last one the Mega Ball Number called. Then save the file again and keep the name of 'Stats.txt'. Any editing you need to do now can easily be done with Notepad which comes with any Microsoft Operating System. 'Stats.txt' will be the hard coded file name the Visual Prolog application will expect – part of avoiding to have the user type information.

If you don't have Microsoft Word or Excel, then use whatever Spreadsheet and Word Processing Applications you have to accommodate the needed changes explained above. Actually, you could do quite a bit with Notepad; however, it does not provide very good features for replacing non-printable characters.

Once you have accomplished the creation of the 'Stats.txt' File to be used to import the needed Historical information, we are now ready to start constructing the Visual Prolog Lottery Application Program.

### 3.3.3 Piecing together the Application Source Code

Go ahead and open Visual Prolog and you will want to start a 'New Project'. You could give the Project Name anything you wish, but for simplicity I will call it GAMegaLotto. While you are in the Dialog Box to name this Project, you will find it to be a very busy Dialog Box with many features that can be defined at the very beginning of your Project Creation. You can explore the various settings under the tabs of General, Directories, Build Options, Version Information, File Templates, and Run Options. However, if you are a beginner I would recommend NOT changing anything right now for this application, unless told to do so. Save any exploration changes for some other Project with personal experimentation as you get more familiar with Visual Prolog. As stated, for Project name use GAMegaLotto and take all the installed defaults provided. This will be an *Object Oriented GUI* UI Strategy, an *Exe* Target Type, Base directory should be under C:\Visual Prolog (or where ever you prefer – mine will probably be different than yours), with a sub-directory of GAMegaLotto. See Figure 3.3.2.a below.

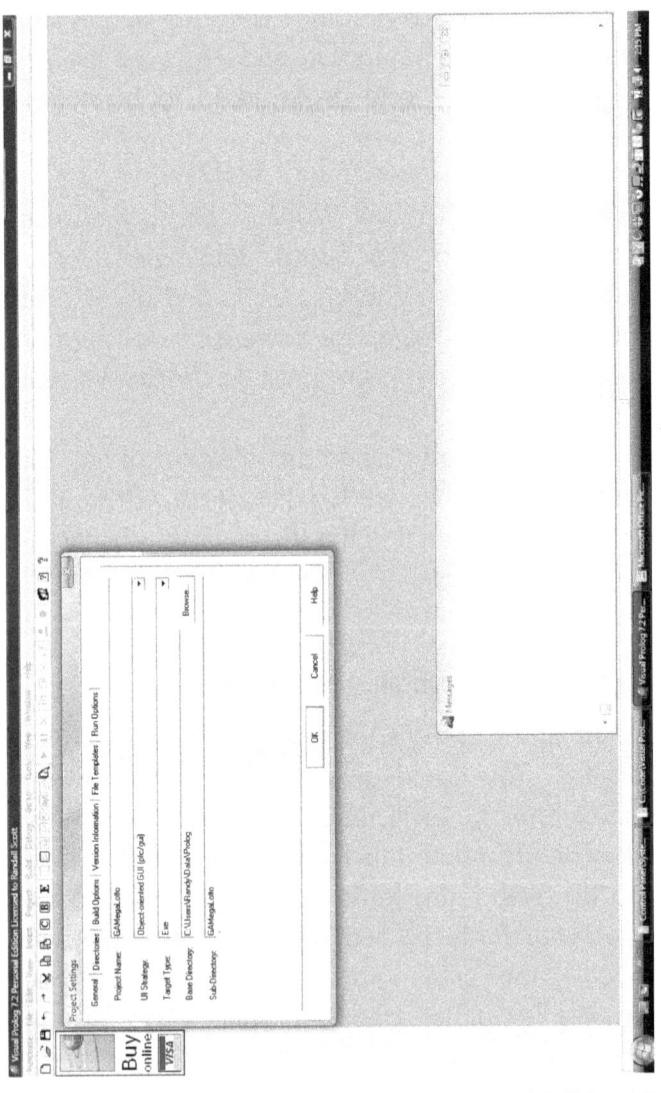

3.3.2.a - Create Project GAMegaLotto (Personal Edition View)

# SAMPLE APPLICATION

Click the OK Button and you will now be in the standard Visual Prolog Integrated Development Environment (IDE). Go ahead and use the Menu option to *Build* the application – this will take a while and you will see a lot of information passed during the process in the Message Window. During the Build process, you will be asked to *add* features. Until you get familiar with all the given PFC features, I recommend you select the 'Add All' option. It will take a while to compile, and when you get to see your Application, you won't be able to do much other than exit the Application either through the Menu or from the upper right X in the window frame.

If you expand the Project Tree (which somewhat resembles Microsoft Explorer), it should look similar to Figure 3.3.2.b. below. And even though what you have so far doesn't do much, you can go ahead and execute it using the menu option Build, submenu Execute (you should notice that you have toolbar buttoms to *Build* and *Execute* as well). Mostly what you will find interesting is what gets created and added to your Project Tree. You can click the items in the Project Tree on the left side to see what is displayed in the right hand portion of the window; or, double click them to open them. The window behavior will be dependent on what they are: source code, resource files, etc. For source files, the right hand window will be very useful to get predefined Prolog Structure information related to Domains, Constants, Facts, and Predicates.

I don't wish to make this book very busy with pictures, so I will refrain from showing pictures (or images) for each step that I explain. However, I will if and when I think it may be useful.

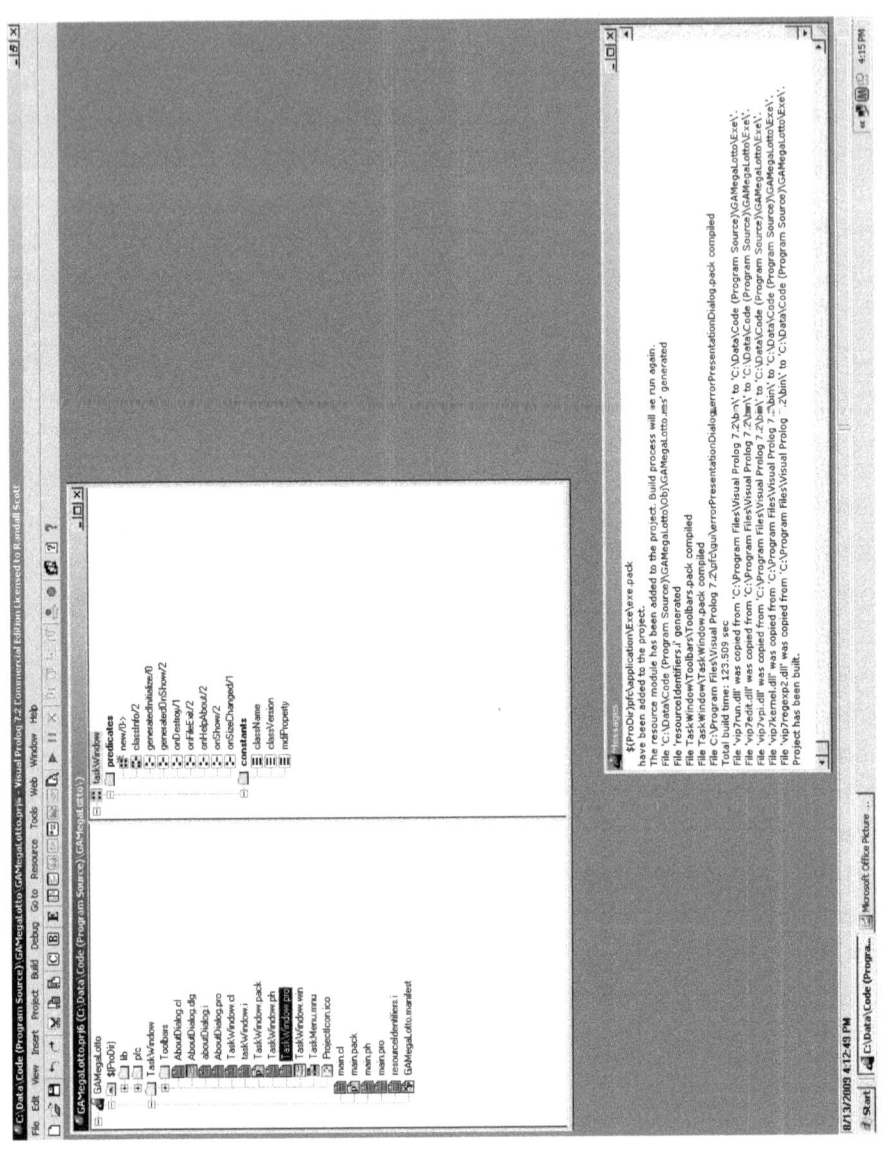

◄ A GUIDE TO ARTIFICIAL INTELLIGENCE WITH VISUAL PROLOG

3.3.2.b - Project Tree (Commercial Edition View)

### 3.3.3.1 Creating a Package for specific Functionality

To gain an appreciation for modularity and scoping we will start by creating a package. The package we wish to create will embody

◄ 42

## SAMPLE APPLICATION

most of the source code for our application's functionality with visibility options tailored for specific modules.

To create a package, make sure GAMegaLotto is selected in the Project Tree, and select menu option 'File', submenu 'New in New Package'. For now on, I will refer to menu and submenu options as follows 'File/New in New Package'. From this Dialog Box you should see everything that you can create with the IDE; from *Package* to *Text File*. Visual Prolog will provide most of the source code for these objects, which in turn you will either use the Code Expert (for source code) or GUI editors to make needed modifications. This can be a 2 edge sword in that it is tremendously convenient for those who understand Visual Prolog and what it does; and, very dangerous for those who are new and don't know how to correct mistakes they make.

At this point I would like to point out the flexibility of the Object 'Text File', as this Object in the Dialog Box can be used to create your own Prolog source files; just make sure you give them the proper filename extensions for Visual Prolog to interpret correctly: '.cl' for Class Declarations, '.pro' for Class Implementations, and '.i' for Interfaces. However, it is much better to just use the 'Class' and 'Interface' Objects to create these as needed, as Visual Prolog will make or modify the needed Package and Header compiler link requirements for you. I recommend leaving '.pack' for Packages and '.ph' for Package Headers for Visual Prolog to create; however, as you get more familiar and advanced, you may need to open them to make necessary corrections depending on what is needed.

For now, select object Package in the left hand portion of the Dialog Box and use the Name of 'Lotto' - take all the other default settings. Click the Create Button and you will notice the 'Lotto' File Folder in your Project Tree with a 'Lotto.pack' file in it. Now compile it using the menu Build option (you don't have to execute it each

43

time you build or compile), and see the package Header File 'Lotto.ph' that gets added to the Lotto folder of the Project Tree.

### 3.3.3.2 Polishing Visual Prolog generated GUI items

Now that we have our Package to work with, we will now start building functional modules for it. However, before we do so, we will setup our Application Menu Options first, for place holders that will point to visible Predicates in our source code in the Lotto Package when activated. To do this we will need to modify the Generic Menu created for our Application by Visual Prolog when we created the Project. Before we modify the Generic Menu, we will define what Menu Options we want to have. This is a careful Design consideration that you will need to go through, to carefully identify those portions not needed as well as those you wish to add. Keep in mind, the Options you choose to remove have significant chunks of source code tied to them, which if you find you removed them by mistake, you may need to start all over with a new Project. The menu and submenu Options we will want are as follows:

    File\Exit
    Import Data
    Get Numbers
    Window\Tile – Cascade - Icon Arrange - Message
    Help\Download Procedure - About

We'll keep the menu option 'File' already created, only for the 'Exit' submenu option – we won't need the other submenu items. Unless you wish to create your own entire Menu, and not reuse features of the one already created, there isn't much you can do to get rid of the 'Window' menu option and its submenus. We'll also keep the one for 'Help' with submenu 'About'; but, we'll add a submenu for 'Download Procedure'. All the other ones we will create.

'Import Data' will be used to do the import of the data

## SAMPLE APPLICATION

downloaded and converted for Visual Prolog importation ('Stats. txt'). It will also be used to analyze the data to get all the desired historical information. External files will be used to store results so this information can be reused until it becomes necessary to redo the download and import.

'Get Numbers' will be used eventually to display the desired historical information as well as acquiring the random Numbers based on both just generic random numbers, and randomly selecting Numbers from the historical data collected.

'Help/Download Procedure' will be handy to explain how to download and convert the Lottery information for importation in case the user forgets - a valid help feature.

As this Application is only an example, you are free to modify it as you wish. You may find other options more useful, or you may wish to expand it. However, again if you are new, I recommend sticking to the example instructions presented first, and then make changes as you get more familiar.

To change the existing already created Menu, do the following:

a. Expand the 'TaskWindow' folder in the Project Tree and find the file named 'taskmenu.mnu'.

b. Double click on the file 'taskmenu.mnu' to enter the Menu GUI Editor for it.

c. Expand all the Menu items so you can see everything that Visual Prolog created for you. We will first remove everything we don't want.

   i. Under '&File' select each entry not wanted one at a time, by clicking on it, then pressing the Delete Key. Delete all of the entries except 'E&xit'. You'll need to remove the dashed line entry as well; however, you'll notice how convenient they can be to separate items in the submenus when the application runs. You'll also notice as you select each one, the 'Disable' check box is marked. After we get all the Menu Options set the way we want, we will activate them one at a time when we get our source code in the Lotto Package ready for them by removing the check mark in the 'Disable' check box, thereby activating or enabling them.

ii. Click on '&Edit' then press the Delete Key. We don't need this menu item or its submenus.

iii. Under '&Help' remove everything under it except '&About'

iv. To create new menu entries or add submenus, we will use the Dialog Box Toolbar. Click on '&File', then click on the Toolbar Button for 'New Item'. In the entry box provided, type '&Import Data'. The Ampersand symbol should under program control cause the character next to it in the Title 'Import Data' to be underlined, which can also be used for the menu selection from the keyboard instead of using the mouse. Search the Visual Prolog Help for 'Properties of GUI Controls' for other useful information pertaining to Menus.

v. Similarly, click on the GUI Editor Toolbar Button for 'New Item' and in the entry box provided type '&Get Numbers'.

vi. For the last menu item click on the '&Help' Then with '&Help' selected, click the toolbar button for 'New SubItem' and in the entry box provided type '&Download Procedure'.

vii. Use the toolbar Arrow Buttons to move the Menu entries into

## SAMPLE APPLICATION

the desired sequence:
   File
      Exit
   Import Data
   Get Numbers
   Help
      Download Procedure
      About

*Note: Be careful in typing these menu item Titles names, as what you type is also used to generate source code. Later, if you don't like the title name and try to change it, it may not be completely changed for all the source code generated.*

You may wish to ensure all the menu entries are deactivated by checking the 'Disable' box for each one. Later when the appropriate source code is created for them, they can be activated at that time.

Go ahead and exit the Menu GUI Editor and save the changes made. To refresh your memory, rebuild and execute the application and check the menu items you modified and added. They should be grayed out to confirm the deactivation; and, you will see the unneeded Toolbar. Also, you will notice the 'Windows' menu item active, which you can not do much about unless you totally remove this menu Visual Prolog created for you and create your own. However, we will keep this one as it provides a good learning tool. Lastly, although you deactivated the '&Exit' menu item, you can still exit the application by clicking on the upper right window frame X. Or, you can go back and activate the '&File' as well as the '&Exit' menu items and confirm their operation after rebuilding and executing.

Below is an image of the GUI Menu editor with all the Menu items added and removed for TaskMenu under TaskWindow.

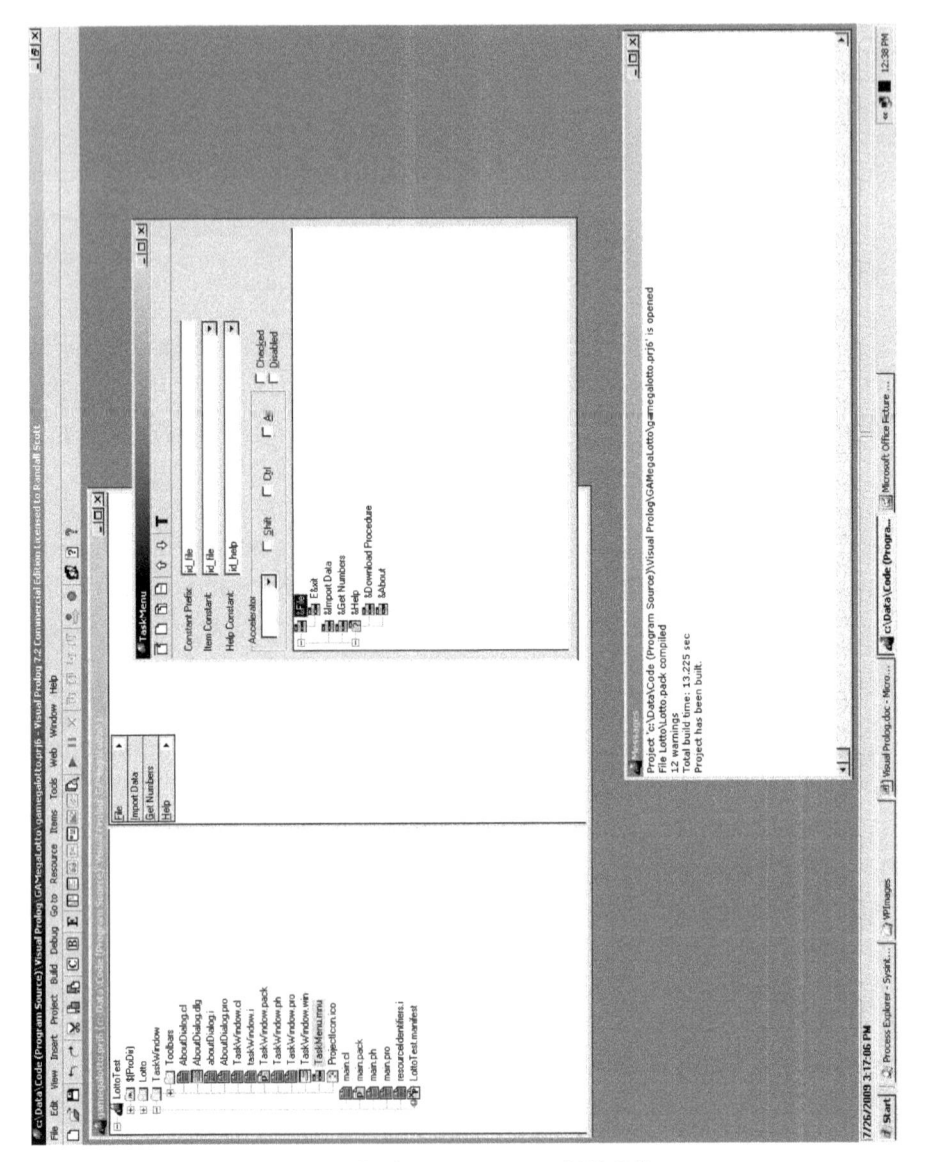

## A GUIDE TO ARTIFICIAL INTELLIGENCE WITH VISUAL PROLOG

**3.3.3.2 - TaskMenu Menu GUI Editor**

One more item we can take care of before proceeding to our Lotto Package source code is to get rid of the generic Toolbar created for this project. If you go to the Project Tree, you will notice a folder named 'Toolbar' right under the folder named 'TaskWindow'. If you expand it out, you will also find a significant list of entries that are

◀ 48

associated with the 'Toolbar' Project Tree folder. For now I don't recommend trying to delete any of these files. We will just remove the Toolbar buttons via the Toolbar GUI Editor.

Locate the file named 'projecttoolbar.tb' and double click on it. When the Toolbar GUI Editor opens, you should see a green vertical insertion marker to the left of the first Toolbar Button (you may need to click on the Insertion Bar to make sure it is active). There are 9 Buttons, as well as 3 vertical Button separators. Just start hitting the Delete Key and watch the Buttons and Vertical Separators disappear. When they are all deleted, exit the GUI editor and save your changes. Now if you rebuild and execute this application, the Toolbar will be gone.

Later on, if you wish to explore putting Toolbar Buttons on this application, the Toolbar is actually still there, just add Buttons and tie your source code to them as needed. For simplicity, I don't plan to use them for this application. I'm sure you can find help in that area from other reference material available. At this point, we can proceed to our functional source code.

### 3.3.3.3 Organizing our Functional Source Code

To begin with, we already mapped a large portion of our design with the menu items we chose, so the first task will be to import the data we downloaded. Once we have the data imported, we will split the functionality to extract the desired historical information, get or display desired Lottery numbers, set up the desired information for printing, and lastly provide some useful User Help. Also, it would be a good idea to start consolidating Constants and Domains that will be needed throughout the application, and to be visible to all modules in our Lotto Package – no need to redefine the same thing every time it's needed. The consolidation will be done by creating a Class which in turn will be a module, because it will not actually create any objects.

# A GUIDE TO ARTIFICIAL INTELLIGENCE WITH VISUAL PROLOG

The first module we will create will contain our desired visible Constants and Domains. Normally, you would incrementally add items to this file as you progress; however, I'll list quite a few and explain their purpose. After that, our focus will shift to the source code related to importing the Lottery Data.

So go to the IDE, make sure you click on the 'Lotto' folder to have it is selected, then select the menu 'File/New in Existing Package' (or, you can right click on 'Lotto' folder and do the same).

The object you will need to select is the one labeled 'Class' by clicking on it. For *Name* use 'LottoDomains'. Uncheck the box for *Create Objects* (which will make it a module), and take the other defaults, followed by clicking the Create Button.

You will notice in the Project Tree, Visual Prolog created 2 new files: 'LottoDomains.cl' (for the Class Declarations) and 'LottoDomains.pro' (for the Class Implementation). It will also have both of these files open for you to Edit - by adding, changing, or deleting source code. Kind of like the Microsoft Notepad Editor; however, as you enter information you will notice some nice features that color code information as you type, and may interact with you by providing message boxes of information, to somewhat ease the burden of some typo errors when entering source code. Actually, the 'LottoDomains.pro' will not be needed for additional source code, but we will leave it alone. The information that you will need to add or enter for Visibility is for the File 'LottoDomains.cl' and will be as follows:

*Right after the following first 2 lines (add % Comments if you wish):*

    class lottoDomains    % Name of the Class
      open core          % Usually needed for everything you create

*Enter:*

## SAMPLE APPLICATION

**domains**                                    % Global Domains to be used
  year = integer.                    % Lotto Data Imported: Year, Month, and Day
  month = integer.
  day = integer.
  number = integer.                  % Generic use of Numbers
  fiveNumbers = integer*.            % List of 5 Numbers
  strList = string*.                 % Generic List of String
  numData = num
  (number,number).                   % Functor to Compound a number with info
  file = input; output.              % Used to deal with files

**constants**

| | | |
|---|---|---|
| lottoReadFile | = "Stats.txt". | % The hard coded name<br>% of the download file |
| localData | = "LocalData.txt". | % Used to Localize Data<br>% for the program |
| lottoDB | = "LottoData.txt". | % Imported Lotto Data in<br>% format used by Prolog |
| lottoCntData | = "NumberCounts.txt". | % Information for<br>% program verificaion<br>% analysis |
| lottoHistory | = "HistoryData.txt". | % Extracted Historical<br>% Information. |
| lottoHelpFile | = "ImportInstructions.hlp". | % File to be used to<br>% provide User Help |
| lottoNumbers | = "LottoNumbers.txt". | % File use to Print History<br>% and Random Numbers |

  % Number Balls  1-56    Numbers used for Regular Lotto Balls
  % Money Ball    1-46    Numbers used for the Mega Money Ball

When you finish entering the information above, exit the editor and save your changes. You don't have to enter all the commented information. In the 'constants' Section, I provided a lot of files we will use to consult, test, and debug our code as we go along. Later, many of these can be eliminated or commented out of your source code when code activity is doing what is desired. You'll see the logic as we progress.

Go ahead and rebuild the application. Now if you select

'LottoDomains.cl' in the Project Tree (left window) you will see the Constants and Domains you created, and a Predicate Visual Prolog created in the right window, without having to go into an editor. Nice and convenient Prolog Structure information. Also, if you open the file 'Lotto.ph' or 'Lotto.pack', you will notice Visual Prolog made the appropriate inclusion entries for the LottoDomains Class for you. If you created the 'LottoDomains.cl' and 'LottoDomains.pro' Class Files using the 'Text File' object, you would manually have to add the '.ph' and '.pack' entries yourself. This can be a clumsy operation trying to make sure the proper entries are made in the '.pack' and '.ph' files for the compiler. A good spot to understand some of the pleasure of what Visual Prolog will do for you.

To summarize a little, every time you create a class, you must deal with the Class Declaration within the '.cl' file as well as the Class Implementation within the '.pro' file. External visibility will be controlled by entries in the '.cl' Class Declaration file and privately in the '.pro' Class Implementation file.

Following the same procedure explained above for creating the 'LottoDomains' module, create another Class (or module) named 'ConvertData'. You should now have 2 more files in the 'Lotto' Folder in the Project Tree with a '.cl' and '.pro' filename extension; with proper entries made in the 'Lotto.ph' and 'Lotto.pack' files. Most of our Source Code will be in these 2 new files to do the data importation and historical analysis.

I could just list all the source code to put in these files, but I think it would be better to incrementally add, explaining as I do. To begin with, we know which file has our data to import ('Stats.txt') and for simplicity we will require it to be located in the same location as the compiled and executable GAMegaLotto program, so we don't have to deal with locating it during execution. However, I will expose you to some useful techniques as we progress. I will start with needed changes (in bold) to the

## SAMPLE APPLICATION

'ConvertData.cl' file which is more visible:

*Before:*
    class convertData
      open core

    predicates
      classInfo : core::classInfo.
      % @short Class information predicate.
      % @detail This predicate represents information predicate of this class.
      % @end

*After:*
    class convertData
      open core, **lottoDomains**

    predicates
      **getData : ().**   % We want this Predicate visible outside of convertData

      classInfo : core::classInfo.
      % @short Class information predicate.
      % @detail This predicate represents information predicate of this class.
      % @end

    *Note: We want access to the Domains and Constants in 'lottoDomains'; as well as access to the predicate 'getData' outside of the Class 'convertData' Class.*

If you try to rebuild now, you'll get an error because the Predicate 'getData' has no Clauses defined for it yet. Don't bother trying to rebuild until I tell you.

Since I know there are a few provided Predicates that I will need, and they don't come with the 'core' (thanks to previously reported compiler errors when I tried to use them), I will include their PFC names as follows with the 'open' statement in the implementation file. So, we will need to make the following changes (in Bold) in the 'ConvertData.pro' file:

*Before:*

>   implement convertData
>       open core

*After:*

>   implement convertData
>       open core, **lottoDomains, string, list**

For what it's worth, as you study Visual Prolog Help and the Reference Manual, you'll find Predicates that you would like to use; and, when you do and compile the program, the Compiler will give you errors if it can't find them. This is where information in the Packages and Package Headers are important as well.

Although not mentioned earlier, in the Project Tree you'll also find a Package ('.pack'), Package Header (.ph'), and Class ('.cl' & '.pro') named 'Main'. In reality, 'Main' is where your program actually begins execution with a Predicate named 'run()' in the Visual Prolog created Goal Section, inside the file 'Main.pro'.

If you look close at the files under PFC in the Project Tree, 'core' is one of them. By using the 'open' statement, Visual Prolog allows the package Domains, Constants, and Predicates to be used within the Class without using external Class Scope identifiers - hence, why you needed to add 'lottoDomains', 'string', and 'list' to 'core' in the 'open' statement. We will be using already provided *string* and *list* manipulation Predicates defined in the PFC, without adding Class Scope Identifiers ('::').

### 3.3.3.4 Import Data

The next task is to import the data from the 'Stats.txt' file that we downloaded and massaged. To do this, we will need to open the file and read the data. As we read it, we will reformat it and place it in an internal database ('class facts') Section that we will give the name of 'lottoData'. When we extract the needed historical

## SAMPLE APPLICATION

information, we will place it in a 'class facts' Section under the name of 'histotyData'. In addition, we will also use 2 other 'class facts' by the names of 'localFacts', and 'lottoNumberData' for program progress, analysis, and debugging.

In the event you are not aware, the nice part of using internal databases (Visual Prolog calls 'class facts' or 'facts'), is that you can save data collected into text files for later consultation, and these files you can use Microsoft Notepad to read. A disadvantage to using 'class facts' or 'facts', is that they are local and visible only to the named Class or Object they are defined in. Therefore if you wish to access them, all your access code will have to reside within the named Class or Object. Visual Prolog provides a way to create 'facts' Sections within an Object created during program execution, but I plan to try and avoid Object Oriented Programming (OOP) for this example. OOP is quite powerful, but also somewhat complex for those new to the field.

So, open the file named 'convertData.pro' and add the following entries right after the 'open' statement. There are 4 'class fact' Sections with separate names, which, if you look closely, should give you a good understanding of some of the information we will be collecting for possible use later on. Variables are very temporary in their ability to retain information - that is were 'class facts' come in very handy.

```
class facts – localFacts        % Used for local static facts
    months: (integer, integer).

class facts – lottoData         % Converted 'Stats.txt' Lotto Data
    lotto : (year Year, month Month, day Day, number DateCP, fiveNumbers
FN, number MoneyBall).

class facts - lottoNumberData   % Temporary data elements used to
                                % extract information
    numberCount : (numData X).  % Lotto Number and it's count
    numberDate : (numData X).   % Lotto Number and it's date
```

## A GUIDE TO ARTIFICIAL INTELLIGENCE WITH VISUAL PROLOG

```
moneyBallCount : (numData X).   % Money Ball Number and it's count
moneyBallDate : (numData X).    % Money Ball Number and it's date
nList : (number* X).            % A list of numbers
ndList : (number* X).           % A list of dates
mbList : (number* X).           % A list of Money Balls Numbers
mbdList : (number* X).          % A list of Money Ball Number dates
nnc : (number* X).              % A list of Numbers not counted
mbnc : (number* X).             % A list of Money Ball Numbers not counted
lcn : (numData* LCN).           % A list of Least Called Numbers
mcn: (numData* MCN).            % A list of Most Called Numbers
lcmb : (numData* A).            % A list Of Least Called Money Balls
mcmb : (numData* C).            % A list of Most Called Money Balls
ocn : (numData* OCN).           % A list of Oldest Called Numbers
ocmb : (numData* A).            % A list of Oldest Called Money Balls

class facts – historyData       % Desired Historical Information
numbersNeverCalled      : (number* X).
moneyBallsNeverCalled   : (number* X).
leastCalledNumbers      : (number* LCN).
mostCalledNumbers       : (number* MCN).
leastCalledMoneyBalls   : (number* A).
mostCalledMoneyBalls    : (number* C).
oldestCalledNumbers     : (number* OCN).
oldestCalledMoneyBalls  : (number* A).
```

In the list above, if you look close at the 'lotto' 'class fact' and compare it to the data in the 'Stats.txt' file, you'll notice it has one more data element for a number with the Variable DateCP. Because Visual Prolog does not provide a means to compare dates (a perverse mixed radix system), we will need to convert the Year, Month, and Day values for each Lotto Number group to something that can be used to compare dates to find the oldest ones. I'll explain the conversion algorithm used when we get to the actual predicates.

So far, we haven't created any Clauses Sections yet; however, before doing so I want to provide a few more Predicates in the 'convertData.pro' Class Implementation file. In the process, I will expose you to use of the Predicate Mode, as well as Paramenter Flows in the Predicate declaration Section. I will also explain the purpose of each Predicate. So, right after the 'class facts' that you entered previously, enter the following Predicate Section (don't forget, that the 'getData' Predicate was already defined in the 'convertData.cl' file and will be visible here as well):

```
% Import Downloaded Data ---------------------
class predicates
    putData : () procedure.
    readData : (inputStream I) procedure (i).
    convStrList : (string Str, strList SL) procedure (i,o).
    getDate : (strList Str, year Y, month M, day D, number N) determ (i,o,o,o,o).
    getFiveNumbers : (strList SL, fiveNumbers N) determ (i,o).
    getMoneyBall : (strList SL, number N) determ (i,o).
    splitLine : (string Lotto, year Year, month Month, day Day, number DateCP,
            fiveNumbers FiveNumbers, number MoneyBall) determ (i,o,o,o,o,o,o).
```

If you have done programming before, you know a lot of functionality tends to come in pairs: if you Read something, you will probably need to Write it too - [Open and Close], [Input and Output], etc. In this case we have a 'getData', so we will also create a 'putData', although our 'putData' functionality will not be similar to the 'getData' in that all it will do is to save our databases to external files. The 'readData' should be somewhat obvious to our importation process; however, if you are somewhat new, I recommend reading more about 'inputStream' as well as 'outputStream' in the Visual Prolog Help.

We will need to convert a String to a String List; or in other words, maybe split a long single String into a list of smaller ones. The 'getDate' Predicate will do the needed conversion I mentioned before. The 'splitLine' Predicate will be the one that actually converts the information read from 'Stats.txt' and make it available to place in the 'lottoData' 'class fact'. The remaining 2 Predicates get the needed Lotto Numbers. When you see the *clauses* Section for these predicates, they should provide a lot more meaning to help you understand.

I'm giving you quite a lot of source code initially at one time as

## A GUIDE TO ARTIFICIAL INTELLIGENCE WITH VISUAL PROLOG

opposed to one predicate and clause definition at a time. I hope you study each predicate with its matching clause definitions, and the sequencing of the calls to appreciate the design. I'll explain more after you make these entries.

So without further ado, enter the following *clauses* Section after the previous *class predicates* Section:

```
% Import Downloaded Data --------------------------------
clauses
   getData() :-
      stdio::write("Reading Downloaded and Converted Data ........\n"),
      I = inputStream_file::openFile8(lottoReadFile),
      readData(I),
      stdio::write("Download Data Acquired ........ \n"),
      % initializeHistoryData,
      % stdio::write("All Numbers, Money Balls, and their Dates have
      % been Initialized ........\n"),
      % getAllNumbers,
      % stdio::write("All Numbers and Money Balls have been Counted
      % ........\n"),
      % stdio::write("All Dates Called have been Normalized ........\n"),
      % getHistory,
      % stdio::write("All Historical Information has been compiled ........\n"),
      putData,
      stdio::write("Data Exported as Consultable Files ........\n\n"), !.
   getData().

   readData(I) :-
      not(I:endOfStream()),
      Lotto = I:readLine(),
      splitLine(Lotto, Year, Month, Day, DateCP, FiveNumbers, MoneyBall),
      assertz(lotto(Year, Month, Day, DateCP, FiveNumbers, MoneyBall)),
      readData(I),
      fail.
   readData(_):-!.

   putData() :-
      % file::save(lottoCntData, lottoNumberData),
      file::save(lottoDB, lottoData),
      file::save(lottoHistory, historyData), !.
```

## SAMPLE APPLICATION

```
splitLine(Lotto, Year, Month, Day, DateCP, FiveNumbers, MoneyBall) :-
    convStrList(Lotto,SL),
    getDate(SL, Year, Month, Day, DateCP),
    getFiveNumbers(SL, FiveNumbers),
    getMoneyBall(SL, MoneyBall), !.

convStrList(Str, [H|T]) :-
    frontToken(Str,H,Str1), ! ,
    convStrList(Str1,T).
convStrList(_,[]).

% --------- M,D,Y,1,2,3,4,5,M -----------
    getDate([X,Y,Z,_,_,_,_,_,_], Year, Month, Day, DateCP) :-
    Month = toTerm(month, X),
    months(Month, Count),
    Day = toTerm(day, Y),
    Year = toTerm(year, Z),
    DateCP = ((Year-2000)*1000) + Count + Day,!.

getFiveNumbers([_,_,_,A,B,C,D,E,_],FiveNumbers) :-
    Z = toTerm(number, A),
    Y = toTerm(number, B),
    X = toTerm(number, C),
    W = toTerm(number, D),
    V = toTerm(number, E),
    FiveNumbers = [Z,Y,X,W,V], !.

getMoneyBall([_,_,_,_,_,_,_,_,X], MoneyBall) :-
    M = toTerm(number, X),
    MoneyBall = M.

months(1, 0).
months(2, 31).
months(3, 60).
months(4, 91).
months(5, 121).
months(6, 152).
months(7, 182).
months(8, 213).
months(9, 244).
months(10, 274).
months(11, 305).
months(12, 335).
```

Clause Section Explanation: Let's start with the 'GetData' Predicate which will eventually be called from the 'Import Data' Menu option. The sequence is to:

- Setup an Input Stream to read the file 'Stats.txt' using the 'lottoReadFile' constant,
- Read each line in the file one line at a time with 'readData()',
- Convert the information to Prolog usable information in the 'lottoData' database, then
- Use the Lotto information to get and put the desired history information in 'lottoHistory'.

I commented out several lines so we can progress incrementally. I also provided lines to send messages to the Message Window so we can watch a little of our program as it executes and evaluate its progress.

At this point, I won't explain all my algorithms in the *clauses* Section and leave them for you to study. Some you may wish to explore using the provided 'PIE' application. Most are fairly straight forward and easy to figure out; and, there may be more elegant solutions for some. You'll also notice I used some already given Visual Prolog Predicates like 'toTerm', 'frontToken' 'fail', '!' (or 'cut'), 'assertz', and 'not'.

I commented out a lot of stuff we will progress to after the import. From some of the commented out material, you should notice we will get to some predicates where Class Scope Identifiers will be used, like for 'stdio' and 'file'. The one for 'inputStream_file' was not commented out. I'll explain more when we get there.

As a suggestion though, I recommend studying the conjunctive predicates listed after the implication of the 'getData' predicate in the *clauses* section. When you get familiar with them, you should only start with one set at a time in the *clauses* sections for specific

SAMPLE APPLICATION

functionality. The easiest way is to comment out everything except the predicates and clauses you want to execute. If it's part of a nested conjunction whose implication is being executed, then don't comment it out. This will allow you to incrementally build functionality, with viewable results in the Message Window; that let you check for correctness as you progress with the program; as well as not putting too much code out there that may confuse you.

For example, the first line sends a message that the download reading process is starting. The next 3 lines set up the input Stream for reading the file 'Stats.txt', calls the predicate 'readData', and when done reports the progress in the message window. Keep in mind when you study the 'readData' predicate in the *clauses* section, it in turn will call the 'splitLine' predicate as well (among other's you did not define in the *clauses* Section), so make sure you include it (i.e. don't comment it out) with the 'readData' set, as you incrementally add code, and as you rebuild and execute. This is a process you should try to get comfortable with as you expand the application. I will be giving you rather large blocks of code as we progress. Adding predicates that aren't called yet can easily be commented out; and, uncommented when the *clauses* Section definitions are complete. If you try this suggestion, please read the paragraph below that explains how you need to activate the menu option so you can execute the application and use the menu option to Import Data.

I guess now is a good time to elaborate some on my Date conversion algorithm. You'll notice I provided some static facts in the *clauses* Section for 'month()'. Assuming every year was a leap year, every day of every year could be counted from 1 to 366 consistently. However that is not the truth, so to convert dates to a number that can be compared to find oldest dates, I take the date Year value and subtract 2000, then take the remaining value and multiply by 1000, then take the starting number from a date Month using 'month()' (assuming every year was a leap year), and add the Day value of the date. I guess you could use the same technique to derive the actual date too (i.e. reverse the process), but I only wanted a way to compare dates, so I calculate this value and include it with the other Lotto data. One last comment, I will be using the 'stdio::write' function periodically to write information to the Message Window, so we can see what is going on – a common debug as you go technique. Nice to see what is happening (or not happening), to help know where to look in your code to solve some problems.

Well, one more step and we can actually rebuild the application and start seeing some functionality working. Go to the Project Tree and locate the 'TaskWindows.win' file. Right Click on it and select the 'Code Expert' (or double click it and push the 'Code Expert' button). Expand the box labeled 'Menu'. Then expand the box labeled 'Task Menu'. Next select the item labeled 'id_import_data', Right Click it and select 'Go to Event Code'; or, just double click it. You should see a Predicate and a Clause for 'onImportData'. Change the Clause section as follows:

Before:
    clauses
      onImportData(_Source, _MenuTag).

After:
    clauses
      onImportData(_Source, _MenuTag) :-
         **convertData::getData().**

Exit the Editor and save your changes. You now have an implication (if) following the 'onImportData' predicate which calls your 'getData' predicate in the 'convertData' class in the 'Lotto' Package.

Next, we need to activate the menu item so it can be executed. So go to the Project Tree and locate the 'TaskMenu.mnu' file and double click it to open it in the Menu GUI Editor. Select '&ImportData' and

## SAMPLE APPLICATION

uncheck the 'Disable' checkbox to enable it. Exit the Editor and save your changes. Now rebuild the application. You may get asked by the compiler to add stuff (maybe from the PFC library or adjustments to the package or header files) – just go ahead and add them. In the compilation process of building, you may get some warnings message (probably for items defined but not used yet), but not any errors. Don't worry about warnings. If you did get errors, recheck all of your typing and study the error messages. When that is cleared up and before executing, make sure you have a copy of the 'Stats.txt' file located in the 'Exe' directory under 'GAMegaLotto' created by Visual Prolog when you created this Project. Remember, we hard coded it in essence not to look anywhere for it. It should by default look for it where the program resides. Now execute it and select the 'Import Data' Menu option. You should get a couple of messages in the Message Window to let you know it imported the data and saved some files. You can open these files using Microsoft Notepad. I let it create the file for History Data, but you won't find anything there yet – we will get there soon. In the other file you will find Lottery data converted so Prolog can use it. Now we can proceed to Data Analysis of the Imported Data.

### 3.3.3.5 Data Analysis

Now that we have our Lottery historical data downloaded and imported, we can now begin to analyze the history. The method I will use is to partially segment the information, to get information related to the Number Counts as well as Number Dates. Keep in mind we have two categories: Regular Numbers (5 each per date which have to be somewhere between 1 and 56), and Money Ball Numbers (1 number for each date which has to be somewhere between 1 and 46) [I left a note concerning these number ranges in the 'LottoDomains.cl' file].

In the 'ConvertData.pro' file you'll notice we created a 'class facts' Section by the name of 'lottoNumberData' with 4 entries

### A GUIDE TO ARTIFICIAL INTELLIGENCE WITH VISUAL PROLOG

for 'numbersCount', 'numberDate', 'moneyBallCount', and 'moneyBallDate'. We will first initialize these to account for every possible Number or MoneyBall, with Counts and Dates initially set to zero using the functor 'num(X, Y)' where X = Number, and Y = Count or Date. After these are initialized, we will iteratively traverse all the imported Lottery Data to get oldest dates for each Number as well as total counts of how often the Numbers were called by category. This will mean adding another predicate and clauses Section for the initialization and counting process. Some people prefer to keep all the predicates close to each other as well as clauses – kind of like only having one Section for each. However, this can sometimes make it inconvenient comparing the declaration to the implementation when they are far apart. The choices are yours; but, always remember that all Computer Languages require that you declare things before you can use them. The needed additional implementation predicates and clauses source code are as follows, (study these closely as I again have taken some liberty in forcing some predicate *mode* and parameter *flow* definitions):

```
% Inititial Data --------------------------------------
class predicates
    initializeHistoryData : ().
    initNumbers : (number X, number Y).
    initMoneyBalls : (number X, number Y).
    getAllNumbers : ().
    fiveNumbers : (fiveNumbers X) determ (i).
    moneyBall : (number X) determ (i).
    dates : (number X, fiveNumbers Y, number Z) determ (i,i,i).
    setNumberDate: (number X, number Y) procedure (i,i).
    setMoneyBallDate : (number X, number Y) procedure (i,i).

% Inititial Data --------------------------------------
clauses
    initializeHistoryData() :-
        initNumbers(1,0),
        initMoneyBalls(1,0),!.

initNumbers(57, _) :-
    stdio::write("Number Counts have been Initialized ........\n"), !.
```

## SAMPLE APPLICATION

```
initNumbers(X, Y) :-
   assertz(numberCount(num(X,Y))),
   assertz(numberDate(num(X,Y))),
   NewX = X + 1,
   initNumbers(NewX, Y).

initMoneyBalls(47, _) :-
   stdio::write("Money Ball Counts have been Initialized ........\n"), !.
initMoneyBalls(X, Y) :-
   assertz(moneyBallCount(num(X,Y))),
   assertz(moneyBallDate(num(X,Y))),
   NewX = X + 1,
   initMoneyBalls(NewX, Y).

getAllNumbers() :-
   lotto(_,_,_,W,X,Y),
   fiveNumbers(X),
   moneyBall(Y),
   dates(W,X,Y),
   fail.
getAllNumbers() :- !.

fiveNumbers([A,B,C,D,E]) :-
   retract(numberCount(num(A,OldC1))),
   NewC1 = OldC1 + 1,
   assertz(numberCount(num(A,NewC1))),
   %-----------------------------------------
   retract(numberCount(num(B,OldC2))),
   NewC2 = OldC2 + 1,
   assertz(numberCount(num(B,NewC2))),
   %-----------------------------------------
   retract(numberCount(num(C,OldC3))),
   NewC3 = OldC3 + 1,
   assertz(numberCount(num(C,NewC3))),
   %-----------------------------------------
   retract(numberCount(num(D,OldC4))),
   NewC4 = OldC4 + 1,
   assertz(numberCount(num(D,NewC4))),
   retract(numberCount(num(E,OldC5))),
   NewC5 = OldC5 + 1,
   assertz(numberCount(num(E,NewC5))),!.

moneyBall(A):-
   retract(moneyBallCount(num(A,X))),
```

```
        Y = X+1,
        assertz(moneyBallCount(num(A,Y))),!.

    dates(Date,[A,B,C,D,E],MB):-
        setNumberDate(Date, A),
        setNumberDate(Date, B),
        setNumberDate(Date, C),
        setNumberDate(Date, D),
        setNumberDate(Date, E),
        setMoneyBallDate(Date,MB).

    setNumberDate(Date1, X) :-
        numberDate(num(X, DateO)),
        Date1 > DateO,
        retract(numberDate(num(X, DateO))),
        assertz(numberDate(num(X, Date1))),!.
    setNumberDate(_, _) :- !.

    setMoneyBallDate(Date1, X) :-
        moneyBallDate(num(X, DateO)),
        Date1 > DateO,
        retract(moneyBallDate(num(X, DateO))),
        assertz(moneyBallDate(num(X, Date1))),!.
    setMoneyBallDate(_, _) :- !.
```

The algorithms used are fairly straight forward to minimize how often the imported data is looked at to Count each Number; as well as deriving the oldest dates by comparing them to the ones already stored in our 'facts' database (why every one was initialized to zero). Go ahead and place this source code in the 'ConvertData.pro' file.

Since we have added quite a bit more functionality, go ahead and go to the 'getData' predicate and remove the Comment ' %' character for all the lines of source code previous to the 'getHistory' predicate call. Also, go to the 'putData' predicate and remove the Comment '%' character to activate an additional file to be saved for later viewing. Now rebuild the application and Execute it. You should get fewer warnings (which were actually associated with a lot of the stuff that was previously commented out); however, if you get

# SAMPLE APPLICATION

any compiler errors, recheck your typing.

When you Execute and click on the 'Import Data' Menu option, you should see quite a few more messages in the Message Window.

**Message Window**
    Reading Downloaded and Converted Data ........
    Download Data Acquired ........
    Number Counts have been Initialized ........
    Money Ball Counts have been Initialized ........
    All Numbers, Money Balls, and their Dates have been Initialized ........
    All Numbers and Money Balls have been Counted ........
    All Dates Called have been Normalized ........
    Data Exported as Consultable Files ........

I set these up so you could incrementally track everything we're trying to accomplish in our source code. If you're having difficulty, follow the sequence of the calls and comment out everything new except the pieces (predicates and clauses) you want to watch. If everything seems to work so far, go ahead and exit the application and check in the 'Exe' directory for the files the program saved. You can open these with Microsoft Notepad. They should resemble the traditional Prolog Internal Consultable Databases, and start with a *clauses* Section title. The contents should give you an idea of how our program extracted the needed Counts and Dates for the Lotto Numbers. Later on, you may wish to Comment out some of the messages going to the Message Window, which are currently only being used to assist us to diagnostically check out program progress as it grows in size. Another nice technique for diagnostic analysis of program execution, is to set 'break points' at spots in the source code that will pause execution so you can view what Variables are holding as well as Facts. So between the Debug features and messages sent to the Message Window, you have some great tools at your disposal to monitor and repair your source code. Below is a good example of using Break Points and the Visual Prolog Debug feature.

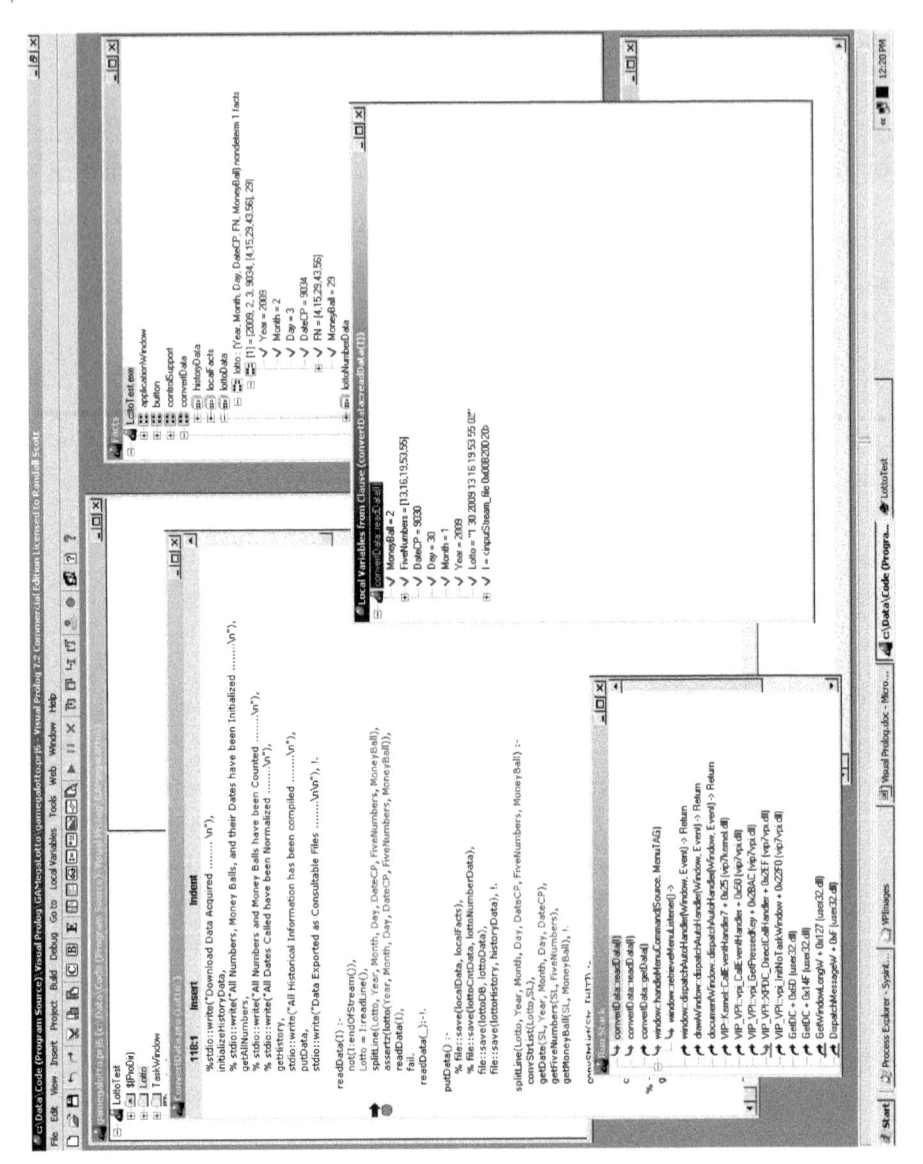

◄ A GUIDE TO ARTIFICIAL INTELLIGENCE WITH VISUAL PROLOG

3.3.3.5 - Visual Prolog Break Point and Debug

One comment about Prolog Internal Databases ('facts' or 'class facts'), is that we used 'asserta' and 'assertz' to place items in it, either at the beginning or at the end. We used the 'retract' predicate to remove items. These databases have no built-in predicates to sort them. So you will probably notice in the 'NumberCounts.txt'

◄ 68

## SAMPLE APPLICATION

file that the Regular Numbers and Money Ball Numbers Counts and Dates are not in numerical order, even though we initially put then in numerical order based on the Number. That was caused by the 'retract' and 'assert' called to replace numbers with their proper Counts and Dates. You'll also notice for the Dates, the converted date number was used, and can be used somewhat like an index to get the real Date when needed, from the 'lottoData' 'facts' database. If you want to do Database functionality that actually supports sorted Databases, then I suggest you procure the Commercial Version of Visual Prolog which will give you many more options.

If you haven't figured it out yet, another nice use of sending messages to the Message Window is to watch your program as it runs. If you wrote some source code to send messages to the Message Window, didn't get any compiler errors, and the messages didn't show up or send information you expected – then you know were in your code to look for the potential problems.

Ok, almost there. All that is left for the intellectual work is to produce the desired results.

### 3.3.3.6 Producing Results

In producing the desired results, we will settle for a fixed range of values so as not to leave the application too open ended. Later, you can make your own adjustments for whatever you desire. For now, I will reduce what we are looking for to only 10 numbers for each category: Regular Numbers never called, least called Regular Numbers, most called Regular Numbers, oldest called Regular Numbers, Money Balls never called, least called Money Balls, most called Money Balls, and oldest called Money Balls. We will start this extraction using the Predicate 'getHistory'.

Again, this will mean adding another predicate and clause definitions to the growing 'ConvertData.pro' file. As you will see,

### A GUIDE TO ARTIFICIAL INTELLIGENCE WITH VISUAL PROLOG

there is quite a bit of source code to add to get this part of the functionality finished. Go ahead and add the following source code. Be as careful as possible to avoid typographical errors. You will notice that I extracted needed items into lists, which in turn were sorted to extract the 10 items of interest.

```
% Get Significant Historical Data (i.e. Never Called, Most Called, Least
% Called, Oldest, etc. --------------
class predicates
  getHistory : ().
  getLists : ().
  getNumbersNeverCalled : ().
  getMoneyBallsNeverCalled : ().
  getExtremeCalledNumbers : ().
  getExtremeCalledMoneyBalls : ().
  getOldestNumbers : ().
  getOldestMoneyBall : ().
  getTop10Numbers : (number* L, number* M).
  getTop10MoneyBalls : (number* L, number* M).
  getTop10OldestNumbers : (number* L).
  getTop10OldestMoneyBalls : (number* L).

% Get Significant Historical Data (i.e. Most Called, Least Called, Oldest,
% etc. --------------
clauses
  getHistory() :-
    getLists,
    getNumbersNeverCalled,
    getMoneyBallsNeverCalled,
    getExtremeCalledNumbers,
    getExtremeCalledMoneyBalls,
    getOldestNumbers,
    getOldestMoneyBall, !.

  getLists():-
    findall(W, numberCount(num(_,W)), List1),
    findall(X, numberDate(num(_,X)), List2),
    findall(Y, moneyBallCount(num(_,Y)), List3),
    findall(Z, moneyBallDate(num(_,Z)), List4),
    assertz(nList(List1)),
    assertz(ndList(List2)),
    assertz(mbList(List3)),
```

## SAMPLE APPLICATION

```
        assertz(mbdList(List4)), !.

   getNumbersNeverCalled() :-
        findall(N, (numberCount(num(N, C)), C=0), List),
        assert(nnc(List)),
        assert(numbersNeverCalled(List)).

   getMoneyBallsNeverCalled():-
        findall(N, (moneyBallCount(num(N, C)), C=0), List),
        assert(mbnc(List)),
        assert(moneyBallsNeverCalled(List)).

getExtremeCalledNumbers():-
     retract(nList(C)),
     L = list::sort(C, ascending),
     M = list::sort(C, descending),
     getTop10Numbers(L, M),!.
getExtremeCalledNumbers():-!.

getExtremeCalledMoneyBalls() :-
     retract(mbList(C)),
     L = list::sort(C, ascending),
     M = list::sort(C, descending),
     getTop10MoneyBalls(L, M),!.
     getExtremeCalledMoneyBalls().

getOldestNumbers() :-
     retract(ndList(C)),
     L = list::sort(C, descending),
     getTop10OldestNumbers(L),!.
getOldestNumbers().

getOldestMoneyBall() :-
     retract(mbdList(C)),
     L = list::sort(C, descending),
     getTop10OldestMoneyBalls(L),!.
getOldestMoneyBall().

getTop10Numbers([L1, L2, L3, L4, L5, L6, L7, L8, L9, L10 | _],
              [M1, M2, M3, M4, M5, M6, M7, M8, M9, M10|_] ) :-
     numberCount(num(A1, L1)),
     numberCount(num(A2, L2)),
     A1 <> A2,
     numberCount(num(A3, L3)),
```

## A GUIDE TO ARTIFICIAL INTELLIGENCE WITH VISUAL PROLOG

```
            A3 <> A2, A3 <> A1,
            numberCount(num(A4, L4)),
            A4 <> A3, A4 <> A2, A4 <> A1,
            numberCount(num(A5, L5)),
            A5 <> A4, A5 <> A3, A5<> A2, A5 <> A1,
            numberCount(num(A6, L6)),
            A6 <> A5,
            numberCount(num(A7, L7)),
            A7 <> A6,
            numberCount(num(A8, L8)),
            A8 <> A7,
            numberCount(num(A9, L9)),
            A9 <> A8,
            numberCount(num(A10, L10)),
            A10 <> A9,
            LCNL  = [num(A1, L1), num(A2, L2), num(A3, L3), num(A4, L4),
                     num(A5, L5), num(A6, L6), num(A7, L7), num(A8, L8),
                     num(A9, L9), num(A10, L10)],
            LCNS  = [A1, A2, A3, A4, A5, A6, A7, A8, A9, A10],
            assertz(lcn(LCNL)),
            assertz(leastCalledNumbers(LCNS)),
            numberCount(num(B1, M1)),
            numberCount(num(B2, M2)),
            B1 <> B2,
            numberCount(num(B3, M3)),
            B3 <> B2, B3 <> B1,
            numberCount(num(B4, M4)),
            B4 <> B3, B4 <> B2, B4 <> B1,
            numberCount(num(B5, M5)),
            B5 <> B4, B5 <> B3, B5 <> B2, B5 <> B1,
            numberCount(num(B6, M6)),
            B6 <> B5,
            numberCount(num(B7, M7)),
            B7 <> B6,
            numberCount(num(B8, M8)),
            B8 <> B7,
            numberCount(num(B9, M9)),
            B9 <> B8,
            numberCount(num(B10, M10)),
            B10 <> B9,
            MCNL  = [num(B1, M1), num(B2, M2), num(B3, M3), num(B4,
                     M4), num(B5, M5), num(B6, M6), num(B7, M7), num(B8,
                     M8), num(B9, M9), num(B10, M10)], MCNS  = [B1, B2,
                     B3, B4, B5, B6, B7, B8, B9, B10],
```

## SAMPLE APPLICATION

```
        assertz(mcn(MCNL)),
        assertz(mostCalledNumbers(MCNS)), !.
getTop10Numbers(_,_).

getTop10MoneyBalls([L1, L2, L3, L4, L5, L6, L7, L8, L9, L10 | _],
                   [M1, M2, M3, M4, M5, M6, M7, M8, M9, M10 | _]) :-
    moneyBallCount(num(A1, L1)),
    moneyBallCount(num(A2, L2)),
    A1 <> A2,
    moneyBallCount(num(A3, L3)),
    A3 <> A2, A3 <> A1,
    moneyBallCount(num(A4, L4)),
    A4 <> A3, A4 <> A2, A4 <> A1,
    moneyBallCount(num(A5, L5)),
    A5 <> A4, A5 <> A3, A5 <> A2, A5 <> A1,
    moneyBallCount(num(A6, L6)),
    A6 <> A5,
    moneyBallCount(num(A7, L7)),
    A7 <> A6,
    moneyBallCount(num(A8, L8)),
    A8 <> A7,
    moneyBallCount(num(A9, L9)),
    A9 <> A8,
    moneyBallCount(num(A10, L10)),
    A10 <> A9,
    LCMBL = [num(A1, L1), num(A2, L2), num(A3, L3), num(A4, L4),
             num(A5, L5), num(A6, L6), num(A7, L7), num(A8, L8),
             num(A9, L9), num(A10, L10)],
    LCMBS = [A1, A2, A3, A4, A5, A6, A7, A8, A9, A10],
    assertz(lcmb(LCMBL)),
    assertz(leastCalledMoneyBalls(LCMBS)),

    moneyBallCount(num(B1, M1)),
    moneyBallCount(num(B2, M2)),
    B1 <> B2,
    moneyBallCount(num(B3, M3)),
    B3 <> B2, B3 <> B1,
    moneyBallCount(num(B4, M4)),
    B4 <> B3, B4 <> B2, B4 <> B1,
    moneyBallCount(num(B5, M5)),
    B5 <> B4, B5 <> B3, B5 <> B2, B5 <> B1,
    moneyBallCount(num(B6, M6)),
    B6 <> B5,
    moneyBallCount(num(B7, M7)),
```

## A GUIDE TO ARTIFICIAL INTELLIGENCE WITH VISUAL PROLOG

```
        B7 <> B6,
        moneyBallCount(num(B8, M8)),
        B8 <> B7,
        moneyBallCount(num(B9, M9)),
        B9 <> B8,
        moneyBallCount(num(B10, M10)),
        B10 <> B9,
        MCMBL  = [num(B1, M1), num(B2, M2), num(B3, M3), num(B4,
                    M4), num(B5, M5), num(B6, M6), num(B7, M7), num(B8,
                    M8), num(B9, M9), num(B10, M10)],
        MCMBS  = [B1, B2, B3, B4, B5, B6, B7, B8, B9, B10],
        assertz(mcmb(MCMBL)),
        assertz(mostCalledMoneyBalls(MCMBS)), !.
getTop10MoneyBalls(_,_).

getTop10OldestNumbers([L1, L2, L3, L4, L5, L6, L7, L8, L9, L10 | _]):-
        numberDate(num(A1, L1)),
        numberDate(num(A2, L2)),
        A1 <> A2,
        numberDate(num(A3, L3)),
        A3 <> A2, A3 <> A1,
        numberDate(num(A4, L4)),
        A4 <> A3, A4 <> A2, A4 <> A1,
        numberDate(num(A5, L5)),
        A5 <> A4, A5 <> A3, A5 <> A2, A5 <> A1,
        numberDate(num(A6, L6)),
        A6 <> A5,
        numberDate(num(A7, L7)),
        A7 <> A6,
        numberDate(num(A8, L8)),
        A8 <> A7,
        numberDate(num(A9, L9)),
        A9 <> A8,
        numberDate(num(A10, L10)),
        A10 <> A9,
        OCNL  = [num(A1, L1), num(A2, L2), num(A3, L3), num(A4, L4),
                    num(A5, L5), num(A6, L6), num(A7, L7), num(A8, L8),
                    num(A9, L9), num(A10, L10)],
        OCNS  = [A1, A2, A3, A4, A5, A6, A7, A8, A9, A10],
        assertz(ocn(OCNL)),
        assertz(oldestCalledNumbers(OCNS)),!.
getTop10OldestNumbers(_).

getTop10OldestMoneyBalls([L1, L2, L3, L4, L5, L6, L7, L8, L9, L10 | _]):-
```

## SAMPLE APPLICATION

```
        moneyBallDate(num(A1, L1)),
        moneyBallDate(num(A2, L2)),
        A1 <> A2,
        moneyBallDate(num(A3, L3)),
        A3 <> A2, A3 <> A1,
        moneyBallDate(num(A4, L4)),
        A4 <> A3, A4 <> A2, A4 <> A1,
        moneyBallDate(num(A5, L5)),
        A5 <> A4, A5 <> A3, A5 <> A2, A5 <> A1,
        moneyBallDate(num(A6, L6)),
        A6 <> A5,
        moneyBallDate(num(A7, L7)),
        A7 <> A6,
        moneyBallDate(num(A8, L8)),
        A8 <> A7,
        moneyBallDate(num(A9, L9)),
        A9 <> A8,
        moneyBallDate(num(A10, L10)),
        A10 <> A9,
        OCMBL = [num(A1, L1), num(A2, L2), num(A3, L3), num(A4, L4),
                num(A5, L5), num(A6, L6), num(A7, L7), num(A8, L8),
                num(A9, L9), num(A10, L10)],
        OCMBS = [A1, A2, A3, A4, A5, A6, A7, A8, A9, A10],
        assertz(ocmb(OCMBL)),
        assertz(oldestCalledMoneyBalls(OCMBS)), !.
    getTop10OldestMoneyBalls(_).
```

I'll admit some of the code above is not very elegant, but it works sufficiently. You may have better approaches to the algorithms pursued. Also, you may be wondering why I used a database entry for Numbers Never Called. The reason is for a Lottery System that has as much data generated already like for this one, if we actually got any Numbers Never Called, then maybe it would help point to a flaw in the program.

At this point, go to the 'getData' clause and remove the last 2 Comment '%' characters to activate the 2 lines of source code for 'getHistory' and the Message Window message. Also, I recommend going back to the 'Exe' directory and removing all the '.txt' files except the one labeled 'Stats.txt'. Then rebuild the application and if everything compiles without errors, go ahead and execute it. When you click on the 'Import Data' Menu option now, you should see a new message in the Message Window. Now go to the 'Exe' directory and open the '.txt' files created. All of them should look similar to what you had before; however, now the one called 'HistoryData.txt' has the information we wanted.

**Message Window**
    Reading Downloaded and Converted Data ........
    Download Data Acquired ........
    Number Counts have been Initialized ........
    Money Ball Counts have been Initialized ........
    All Numbers, Money Balls, and their Dates have been Initialized ........
    All Numbers and Money Balls have been Counted ........
    All Dates Called have been Normalized ........
    All Historical Information has been compiled ........
    Data Exported as Consultable Files ........

Take some time to study the algorithms used. I tried to expose you to features associated with visibility – primarily with class modules. Some visibility was accommodated through the 'open' statement; others were accessed using the class identifier 'class::' method. Sometimes using the class identifier methods makes it easier to find code you wish to modify as your application grows in size. Also, sometimes with a growingly large Application, you may find duplication of predicate names with differing parameters and functionality, where use of class identifier clearly helps avoid confusion.

### 3.3.3.7 Clean up

If you are satisfied with the current progress, you can either eliminate or comment out some or all of the Messages sent to the Message Window. What is quite nice about the Message Window that Visual Prolog creates for you, is that at any time you can right click in the Message Window and the Popup Menu will allow you to clear all the Messages. I'm going to comment out all of the messages except the ones indicating the Import Process, as well as Historical Data Collection and Consultable files saved. These you should find with the clauses 'getData', 'initNumbers', and 'initMoneyBalls'. In the process of commenting out the messages in 'initNumbers' and 'initMoneyBalls', don't forget the 'std::write' (message) is the only right hand portion of the first implication; so you will need to add a Cut after the implication with a Period, which preceeds the commented line. The remaining messages are still convenient for an unknowing user. I'm also going to comment out saving 'lottoNumberData' in file 'NumberCounts.txt', under the clause 'putData'; this was only saved to help diagnostically check program correctness. When you rebuild the application, you should only get Warning messages from the compiler mainly because of our comment out activity. Warnings are not a problem; however, if you get Errors recheck all the changes you made.

**Message Window**
   Reading Downloaded and Converted Data ........
   All Historical Information has been compiled ........
   Data Exported as Consultable Files ........

Before we proceed to the Finishing Touches section, we need to think a little about how we accomplished our desired results and some possible side effects. So far we have assumed this is the first time this Application is run. First we initially hand massaged the data to import; then imported the data and in the process extracted the history information we wanted. If this is Not the first time the Application is run, then maybe we would like to just extract the desired history information without having to import it again — save the import process when we want to update it with new Lotto information.

That is also why we created a menu option to Get Numbers. We'll create another module (Class) by the name of 'GetNumbers' and tie some of the get History functionality to it. Keep in mind the database for the information is in the 'ConvertData' module and is not directly accessible from this new 'GetNumbers' module. So, we'll create a predicate in the 'ConvertData' module that is visible and can provide a way to get the information we want out of the history database. We also need to provide some alternative functionality such that if the history data already exists, just get the data. However, we also need a check point such that if the data has not been imported to get the history data, let the user know in the Message Window. So logically, we need to create predicates such that the truth search will be defined in the following sequence: make sure data has been imported by looking for the database file created and saved to store the history data 'HistoryData.txt'. If the data has <u>not</u> been imported with the history collected and saved, this should cause failure and justify sending a message to the Message Window. If it succeeds, then try to get the history data from the internal database. In doing so, if this fails, then consult the 'HistoryData.txt' database to get the history data. This usually will occur when you first start the Application and select the 'Get Numbers' Menu option right away – a way to reuse history information collected already.

This is where you use the same procedure you did before in creating the classes (modules) 'LottoDomains' and 'ConvertData', to create the new one called 'GetNumbers'.

Go ahead and rebuild the application after creating the new module (class) to get the somewhat empty definitions integrated with the application. At least now you will see Predicates in the Project Tree when you select the new module. Next make the necessary additions so the class declaration and implementation look as follows.

The Class GetNumbers.cl should look like:

```
class getNumbers
    open core, lottoDomains, convertData
```

## SAMPLE APPLICATION

```
predicates
  history : () .
  classInfo : core::classInfo.
  % @short Class information  predicate.
  % @detail This predicate represents information predicate of this class.
  % @end

end class getNumbers
```

The Implementation GetNumbers.pro should look like:

```
implement getNumbers
  open core, lottoDomains, convertData

constants
  className = "Lotto/getNumbers".
  classVersion = "".

clauses

  history ():-
    getHistoryData(LCN, LCMB, MCN, MCMB, OCN, OCMB, NCN, NCMB),
    stdio::write("Least Called Numbers     : ", LCN, "\n"),
    stdio::write("Least Called Money Balls : ", LCMB, "\n"),
    stdio::write("Most Called Numbers      : ", MCN, "\n"),
    stdio::write("Most Called Money Balls  : ", MCMB, "\n"),
    stdio::write("Oldest Called Numbers    : ", OCN, "\n"),
    stdio::write("Oldest Called Money Balls: ", OCMB, "\n"),
    stdio::write("Never Called Numbers     : ", NCN, "\n"),
    stdio::write("Never Called Money Balls : ", NCMB, "\n\n\n"), !.
  history ().

  classInfo(className, classVersion).

end implement getNumbers
```

As you can see, we added a Predicate called 'history', which is visible (defined in the class declaration file '.cl'); and, temporarily we are providing a way to put messages to the Message Window to show results.

Now we need to revisit the 'ConvertData' module and create the visible 'getHistoryData' Predicate to get the history data we want. The class ConvertData.cl should now look as follows:

```
class convertData
    open core, lottoDomains

predicates
    getData : ().
    getHistoryData : (number*, number*, number*, number*, number*, number*, number*, number*)
        determ (o,o,o,o,o,o,o,o).

classInfo : core::classInfo.
% @short Class information predicate.
% @detail This predicate represents information predicate of this class.
% @end

end class convertData
```

You'll need to add the following predicate definition to the clauses section of ConvertData.pro. I placed it right at the beginning and before the 'getData' clause.

```
getHistoryData(LCN, LCMB, MCN, MCMB, OCN, OCMB, NCN, NCMB) :-
    numbersNeverCalled(NCN),
    moneyBallsNeverCalled(NCMB),
    leastCalledNumbers(LCN),
    mostCalledNumbers(MCN),
    leastCalledMoneyBalls(LCMB),
    mostCalledMoneyBalls(MCMB),
    oldestCalledNumbers(OCN),
    oldestCalledMoneyBalls(OCMB), !.
```

Now don't forget to go to the Menu Editor and activate the 'Get Numbers' menu option. Then have the menu option call the visible 'history' predicate defined in 'GetNumbers'.

## SAMPLE APPLICATION

### TaskWindow.pro Abstract

```
predicates
    onGetNumbers : window::menuItemListener.
clauses
    onGetNumbers(_Source, _MenuTag) :-
        getNumbers::history(), !.
```

When this is complete, go ahead and rebuild the application and try executing it. If you get any errors, recheck all of your spelling. Again, don't worry about Warnings. Now you should see the history information in the Message Window when you select the 'Get Numbers' menu option.

### Message Window

```
Reading Downloaded and Converted Data ........
All Historical Information has been compiled ........
Data Exported as Consultable Files ........

Least Called Numbers       : [56,55,54,53,33,23,34,47,4,11]
Least Called Money Balls   : [28,19,16,11,16,11,45,31,45,31]
Most Called Numbers        : [14,51,52,39,32,46,10,31,36,16]
Most Called Money Balls    : [21,34,36,35,10,3,38,3,38,4]
Oldest Called Numbers      : [3,6,43,51,3,8,21,8,17,40]
Oldest Called Money Balls  : [36,2,13,41,4,28,31,34,16,9]
Never Called Numbers       : []
Never Called Money Balls   : []
```

Keep in mind, right now, this will only work if you select the 'Get Numbers' menu item immediately after selecting the 'Import Data' menu item. If you try 'Get Numbers' first without an import, you won't get anything.

So as you can see we are not done yet. We still need to do the alternative functions to make sure data has been imported when we select the 'Get Numbers' menu option. To test this functionality, you need to delete all the '.txt' files except the one named 'Stats.txt'. We'll look for the one named 'HistoryData.txt' for our logic test; and

### A GUIDE TO ARTIFICIAL INTELLIGENCE WITH VISUAL PROLOG

we'll expand the source in the 'GetNumbers.pro' implementation file. It should now look as follows with 3 definitions for 'history()':

```
implement getNumbers

  open core, lottoDomains, convertData

constants
  className = "Lotto/getNumbers".
  classVersion = "".

clauses

  history ():-
    existFile("HistoryData.txt"),
    getHistoryData(LCN, LCMB, MCN, MCMB, OCN, OCMB, NCN, NCMB),
    stdio::write("Least Called Numbers    : ", LCN, "\n"),
    stdio::write("Least Called Money Balls : ", LCMB, "\n"),
    stdio::write("Most Called Numbers     : ", MCN, "\n"),
    stdio::write("Most Called Money Balls  : ", MCMB, "\n"),
    stdio::write("Oldest Called Numbers   : ", OCN, "\n"),
    stdio::write("Oldest Called Money Balls: ", OCMB, "\n"),
    stdio::write("Never Called Numbers    : ", NCN, "\n"),
    stdio::write("Never Called Money Balls : ", NCMB, "\n\n\n"), !.

  history ():-
    existFile("HistoryData.txt"),
    getHistoryDataAgain,
    getHistoryData(LCN, LCMB, MCN, MCMB, OCN, OCMB, NCN, NCMB),
    stdio::write("Least Called Numbers    : ", LCN, "\n"),
    stdio::write("Least Called Money Balls : ", LCMB, "\n"),
    stdio::write("Most Called Numbers     : ", MCN, "\n"),
    stdio::write("Most Called Money Balls  : ", MCMB, "\n"),
    stdio::write("Oldest Called Numbers   : ", OCN, "\n"),
    stdio::write("Oldest Called Money Balls: ", OCMB, "\n"),
    stdio::write("Never Called Numbers    : ", NCN, "\n"),
    stdio::write("Never Called Money Balls : ", NCMB, "\n\n\n"), !.

  history ():-
    stdio::write("Data Has Not been imported - Import data First \n\n" ), !.

  classInfo(className, classVersion).

end implement getNumbers
```

# SAMPLE APPLICATION

Also need to add a visible 'getHistoryDataAgain' Predicate in the 'ConvertData.cl' module so we can perform a 'consult' to repopulate the internal 'historyData' database. In addition, we need to add 'file' to the 'ConvertData.pro' open statement for the 'consult' call.

Here are some abstracts of the 'ConvertData' module.

## ConvertData.cl (abstract)

```
predicates
    getData : ().    % We want this Predicate visible outside of convertData
    getHistoryData : (number*, number*, number*, number*, number*, number*, number*)
    determ (o,o,o,o,o,o,o).
    getHistoryDataAgain : ().
```

## ConvertData.pro (abstract)

```
% To retrieve History Data from outside of the ConvertData Class

getHistoryData(LCN, LCMB, MCN, MCMB, OCN, OCMB, NCN, NCMB) :-
    numbersNeverCalled(NCN),
    moneyBallsNeverCalled(NCMB),
    leastCalledNumbers(LCN),
    mostCalledNumbers(MCN),
    leastCalledMoneyBalls(LCMB),
    mostCalledMoneyBalls(MCMB),
    oldestCalledNumbers(OCN),
    oldestCalledMoneyBalls(OCMB), !.

getHistoryDataAgain() :-
    consult("HistoryData.txt", historyData), !.
```

Finally, we need to add 'file' from the 'pfc' to the 'open' statement in the 'GetNumbers.pro' and 'ConvertData.pro' files. It will also help to make the *existFile* and *consult* predicates more visible. They should look as follows:

**GetNumbers.pro Abstract**
    implement getNumbers
        open core, lottoDomains, convertData, file

**ConvertData.pro Abstract**
    implement convertData
        open core, lottoDomains, string, list, file

Rebuild and execute the Application now to properly check the changes made. Does it create files and report messages as expected? Also, review all the files created again. This methodology seems quite tedious after a while, but it helps to acquire talent for systematically engineering good code.

Finally, another area you may wish to explore or study in the Clean Up process, is to investigate algorithms to make file handling maybe a little friendlier. Such as checking if files already exist in other areas of the application before creating them or opening them or saving them. Sometimes canned code may produce undesired results, like maybe unwanted appending of files or getting unexpected runtime errors. This is also where experience with trial and error can be helpful.

### 3.3.3.8 Finishing Touches

Since pretty much all the hard intellectual portions of the program are complete, all that is really left is to work on Eye Candy to present the results. This can be done by using a Form Object to present the information to our User; and/or being able Print the desired Numbers out. In addition, we are to provide Help for the Import data massaging effort needed. Keep in mind, the toughest portions so far for the functionality was built to execute with the 'Import Data' Menu Option. This is important in that now the 'Import Menu' option only needs to be selected when you need to download a new or updated set of data for importation. Once it has been imported, the 'HistoryData.txt' database can be reused simply by using the *consult* Predicate, which has to reside in 'ConvertData.pro' file, and can be called by a visible Predicate on the outside if necessary; as we did with 'getHistoryDataAgain()'

### 3.3.3.8.1 Creating a Form and changing information on it

We'll start by creating a Form Object using the name of 'Numbers'. In case you forgot, right click on the 'Lotto' folder on the Project Tree and select 'New in existing Package'. Then select the Form Object and name it 'Numbers'. This will give you 4 new items in the Project Tree under 'Lotto': Numbers.cl (class), Numbers.i (interface), Numbers.pro (implementation), and Numbers.frm (form GUI).

After creating this object go ahead and rebuild the Application. After rebuilding it, you will see some significant changes in the Project Tree when you select the new items in the left part of the Project Tree window – new canned Predicates, Facts, and Constants show up on the right hand side.

To activate this Form when you select the 'Get Numbers' Menu option, you will need to add some source code to the TaskWindow.pro file. For help getting there, in the Project Tree double-click on 'TaskWindow.win', then click on the 'Code Expert' Button. Then expand the item labeled 'Menu' (click on the '+' symbol). Do the same for the item labeled 'TaskMenu' under it. Then double click on 'id_get_numbers -> onGetNumbers'. This will take you into the file 'TaskWindow.pro' with the insertion point in the clauses section for the predicate 'onGetNumbers'. When you are finished, the source code should look as follows:

```
predicates
   onGetNumbers : window::menuItemListener.

clauses
   onGetNumbers(_Source, _MenuTag) :-
   Form = numbers::new(This),
   Form:show(),
   getNumbers::history(), !.
```

As you should see, I left the previous code which still sends the history data to the Message Window and added 2 lines for the Form. The first line actually creates the Form and the second displays it on the screen. Now save all your work and when you rebuild the Application and Execute it, you'll see the same history information going to the Message Window; however now this Form shows up too. We'll use this form to provide the Number Information the User is interested in. As we do so, we can stop sending similar information to the Message Window. A good place for duality and testing until your code works as desired. Or you can leave it, that's up to you.

Next we need to work with the Form. First we need to adjust some of the canned features: decide if we need all the provided buttons, make needed changes, then provide our own code to display information on the Form. Some of this will be accomplished with the Form GUI Editor and others with our source code.

Go ahead and double click on the 'Numbers.frm' in the Project Tree to enter the Form GUI Editor. To change some of the canned features, in the provided Properties Window we will change the following:

a. Menu – change from 'unset' to 'TaskMenu'
b. MaximizeBox – change from 'true' to 'false'
c. MinimizeBox – change from 'true' to 'false'

This will allow this Form to be associated with the Menu and disable use of the Maximize and Minimize buttons on the Form Window. Later on you can explore other changes to the properties.

As for the three provided Buttons, I think we only need 2. We'll delete 1 and rename the other two to 'Again' and 'Save'. Later we'll use what was saved for Printing. To exit the Form, we have the 'x' in the upper right corner of the Form. We'll delete the 'Help' button, since we will have a Help option on the Menu. Then we will rename

## SAMPLE APPLICATION

'OK' as 'Again'; and, 'Cancel' as 'Save'.

To delete the 'Help' button, click on it to select it, then go to the Visual Prolog menu and select 'edit' followed by 'delete'. To rename the 'OK' button as 'Again', click on it to select it, then in the Properties Window look for the item labeled Text (on the left side) and change the 'OK' to 'Again' (you get the underscore on the first character by typing an ampersand [&] before the word 'Again'). This allows the application to use the keyboard in addition to the mouse to select the Button item. Also change the Name from 'ok_ctl' to 'again_ctl' in the Properties Window. Now follow the same procedure to rename the 'Cancel' button to 'Save' (i.e., Text for the 'Cancel' button from 'Cancel' to 'Save', Name from 'cancel_ctl' to 'save_ctl'). For now, just drag these 2 buttons to the bottom of the Form and near the center. Latter we may need to change the size of the Form, which is easy by dragging the corners of the Form. Exit and save the Form, then rebuild the application to affect the changes to the source code. If you want, execute it to see the changes made so far.

Now to place information on this Form, we will be using a combination of GUI Tools and writing our own source code. When you double click on 'Numbers.frm' in the Project Tree, it is opened up with a Form GUI Editor. You also have one Properties Window with 2 Toolbars populated with icons for 'Controls' and 'Layout', to go with it. We already used the Properties Window. The 2 Toolbars have icons, to place Controls on the Form you created and to graphically work with the Layout of the Controls. For more information, please refer to the 'Beginners' Guide to Visual Prolog', 'Visual Prolog for Tyros', or consult with the Visual Prolog Help references.

Of the History Data we are working with, I will show you how to place the categories (Least Called Numbers, Most Called Numbers, and Oldest Called Numbers – using 5 Regular Numbers and a Money Ball). I'll also provide 1 set of random numbers for the Least

## A GUIDE TO ARTIFICIAL INTELLIGENCE WITH VISUAL PROLOG

Called Numbers [5 out of 10 Regular Numbers; and, 1 out of 10 Money Balls]); but, also one set of purely random numbers that are not associated with the history data.

To Display the Least Called Numbers as described, we need to place some Static Text Control items on the Form. The left one says 'Least Called Numbers: ' and the right one is a place next to it to actually place the numbers we wish to display; which will be integers converted to a string. We'll do something similar for the Random numbers as well.

On the Controls Toolbar select the 'Static Text' Tool by clicking on it, then move the mouse to the Form and drag the Static Text Control to place it on the Form. In the Properties Window change the Text from 'Static Text' to 'Least Called Numbers: '. Resize it as necessary to display all the text. Then place another 'Static Text' Control to the right of this one about the same size; however, we will not change the Properties Text. On the second Static Text control, make sure the Representation is a 'Fact Variable' as opposed to 'Variable'. We'll write our own source code to change the Text to display our Least Called Numbers on the second Static Text control. Use the Layout Toolbar to make sure both Static Text controls are the same horizontal and vertical size. Take note of the Tool Name 'staticText1_ctl' for the one we made a 'Fact Variable', as we will need this to change the Text display for it in our source code.

Ok, we know pretty much what we want to do, but we need to organize the concept a little for easy implementation. I think another local database to store the strings to display would be a good idea. This will also allow a nice means for saving the information to print it later. However, it will be a little complicated when we want to click the 'Again' button, as this will require that we 'retract' the Random numbers and 'assert' the new Random numbers. Also, if we were to just print the saved file, the order will not always be the same, if the 'Again' button feature is used, as items are always either asserted

# SAMPLE APPLICATION

at the beginning or the end ('assert/asserta' vs. 'assertz'). This will require some more work if you want a pretty Print option: either use nice features offered by the Commercial Version; or, save the information into a '.txt' file which cannot be Consulted, and printed from an outside application like Microsoft Notepad. Because I assume most of the audience is probably using the Personal Version, I'll just save the local database to a consultable '.txt' file and print it from some other application.

We could put this new local database in any module; but, we have to keep in mind it will never have Global visibility, so we will probably have to create one or more visible predicates to access the information external to the module it is placed in. I will place it in the implementation portion of the 'GetNumbers.pro' module. Its name will be 'displayNumbers' and the file we will later save it to will be named 'LottoNumbers.txt'. Add the following to 'GetNumbers.pro' right after the constants section. You'll notice this is very similar to the facts in the 'historyData' database in 'Convertdata.pro'. Because I plan to just print the saved database file, the 'fact' names are quite convenient. In Prolog you can have predicates and facts with the same name; but, with different parameters. Technically, this is also referred to as multiple Arities. In this case, the parameters are from a different domain; and, a few facts were added and removed. I only added the ones I will provide for you; but, the ones provided should give you an idea on how to create others. Also, the last one I chose to number the name as you may wish to construct more later on, as well as explore the possibility of unique random numbers for multiple sets.

## GetNumbers.pro (Abstarct)

```
class facts - displayNumbers
  leastCalledNumbers : (string LCN).
  mostCalledNumbers: (string MCN).
  oldestCalledNumbers : (string OCN).
  leastCalledRandom : (string LCR).
  randomLotto1 : (string RL1).
```

# A GUIDE TO ARTIFICIAL INTELLIGENCE WITH VISUAL PROLOG

If not there already, add the file name 'LottoNumbers.txt' as a constant labeled as 'lottoNumbers' in 'LottoDomains.cl' for visibility; which is a convenient place to place all our defined filenames used by the application. If you ever want to change them, you have a single place to look.

Next we have a need to populate this new database in 2 ways. First to convert and 'assert' the history data converted to strings, then to acquire the random number facts. For the first part, I think the logical approach would be to do the conversion and assertion when the history facts are created to begin with; however, the 'ConvertData.pro' module is quite large now already, and we can easily access the stored facts anyway. So, I will do the history data conversion and assertion in the 'GetNumbers.pro' module which has visibility to the new database as it will be local.

We'll create a predicate named 'historyDataConvert' and use similar parameters used by 'getHistoryData'. We don't need the numbers never called (we only used it to test logic), and we will combine information for both Regular Numbers and Money Balls in our conversion to strings.

We'll also use a predicate under the name of 'convertListToString' to actually do the needed conversions. I'll make the integer-to-string conversions for you for the Least Numbers Called, the Most Numbers Called, and the Oldest Numbers Called; however, initially I'll only display the one for Least Numbers Called so we can incrementally watch progress. So make the following entries to the GetNumbers.pro file.

## GetNumbers.pro (abstract)

```
class predicates
    historyDataConvert : (number*, number*, number*, number*, number*,
        number*) determ (i, i, i, i, i, i).
    convertListToString : (number*, number*, string) determ (i, i, o).
```

## SAMPLE APPLICATION

Next the 'clauses' section will be modified as follows:
clauses

```
history ():-
    existFile("LottoData.txt"),
    getHistoryData(LCN, LCMB, MCN, MCMB, OCN, OCMB, NCN, NCMB),
    historyDataConvert(LCN, LCMB, MCN, MCMB, OCN, OCMB),
    stdio::write("Least Called Numbers      : ", LCN, "\n"),
    stdio::write("Least Called Money Balls : ", LCMB, "\n"),
    stdio::write("Most Called Numbers       : ", MCN, "\n"),
    stdio::write("Most Called Money Balls  : ", MCMB, "\n"),
    stdio::write("Oldest Called Numbers     : ", OCN, "\n"),
    stdio::write("Oldest Called Money Balls: ", OCMB, "\n"),
    stdio::write("Never Called Numbers      : ", NCN, "\n"),
    stdio::write("Never Called Money Balls : ", NCMB, "\n\n\n"), !.

history ():-
    existFile("LottoData.txt"),
    getHistoryDataAgain,
    getHistoryData(LCN, LCMB, MCN, MCMB, OCN, OCMB, NCN, NCMB),
    historyDataConvert(LCN, LCMB, MCN, MCMB, OCN, OCMB),
    stdio::write("Least Called Numbers      : ", LCN, "\n"),
    stdio::write("Least Called Money Balls : ", LCMB, "\n"),
    stdio::write("Most Called Numbers       : ", MCN, "\n"),
    stdio::write("Most Called Money Balls  : ", MCMB, "\n"),
    stdio::write("Oldest Called Numbers     : ", OCN, "\n"),
    stdio::write("Oldest Called Money Balls: ", OCMB, "\n"),
    stdio::write("Never Called Numbers      : ", NCN, "\n"),
    stdio::write("Never Called Money Balls : ", NCMB, "\n\n\n"), !.

history ():-
    stdio::write("Data Has Not been imported - Import data First \n\n" ),!.

historyDataConvert(LCN, LCMB, MCN, MCMB, OCN, OCMB) :-
    convertListToString(LCN, LCMB, S1),
    convertListToString(MCN, MCMB, S2),
    convertListToString(OCN, OCMB, S3),
    assertz(leastCalledNumbers(S1)),
    assertz(mostCalledNumbers(S2)),
    assertz(oldestCalledNumbers(S3)), !.


convertListToString([N1, N2, N3, N4, N5 | _], [MB | _], String) :-
    S1 = concat(toString(N1), ", "),
```

```
S2 = concat(toString(N2), ", "),
S3 = concat(toString(N3), ", "),
S4 = concat(toString(N4), ", "),
S5 = concat(toString(N5), " "),
S6 = concat("- ", toString(MB)),
String = concat(S1, S2, S3, S4, S5, S6), !.
```

Be sure to add 'string' to the 'open' statement to get visibility to 'concat' from the PFC. It should now look as follows:

```
implement getNumbers
    open core, lottoDomains, convertData, file, string
```

If you were following along, I made 3 rules for the call to 'history()'. The first looks to see if History data has already been imported, created, and saved. If so, get it. If not then 'consult' the saved history through the getHistoryDataAgain call. If you can't get it, then it hasn't been imported yet – so send an appropriate Message. I had to duplicate the effort to send messages to the Message Window if failures occurred in the first call. This would look easier if you created another single predicate to print the messages and then call it twice instead.

Slowly as you see progress, you can either comment out or delete the lines which send history information to the Message Window. I'll leave them alone for now.

Before we visit the random number concept, lets put the Least Called Numbers on the Form so we can watch a little progress. To do this, we get the Least Called Numbers string from the displayNumbers database and assign it to the desired Static Text Control on the Form. This will be quite involved as you will see, but a great exercise in getting familiar with visibility issues and passing information between modules and objects; as well as a little exposure to working with objects and their methods.

## SAMPLE APPLICATION

To begin with, we'll have 'string' information in the GetNumbers module that we will want to send to the Numbers Form Object. Keep in mind the Form was actually created in the TaskWindows.pro implementation. To make this happen with 3 different pieces of the puzzle, we will get the string information for the 'Static Text' Control on the Form by calling a visible predicate in the GetNumbers module, then place the string on the 'Static Text' control by a call from the TaskWindow.pro implementation, to a visible Interface Predicate we create in the Numbers.i interface, whose implementation will execute the use of the Object method to place the string. This may sound a little lengthy and confusing, so I'll repeat it with examples of what source code needs to be placed where. Start with the Form Numbers.i *interface*, by adding the following visible Predicate:

```
interface numbers supports formWindow
    open core

predicates
    set_text_from_outside_form : (string).

end interface numbers
```

I tried to use a somewhat memory enhancing predicate name. Next add the following implementation clauses to Numbers.pro (which uses the 'setText' method of the Form Object):

```
clauses
    set_text_from_outside_form(S):-
    staticText1_ctl:setText(S),
    update().                    % to repaint
```

Now we need to make some significant changes to GetNumbers. cl, GetNumbers.pro, and TaskWindow.pro. First we'll make the following change to GetNumbers.cl to change the visible Predicate 'history()' to one that uses a string list as an output parameter for 3 strings in the list. You can change this to accommodate more data latter if you wish. This is mainly to give you exposure and how it is

done (notice the interesting flow parameter provided).
## GetNumbers.cl (abstract)

history : (string*) procedure ([o, o, o]).

Next make the necessary modifications to the GetNumbers.pro so it looks as follows:

## GetNumbers.pro

```
implement getNumbers
  open core, lottoDomains, convertData, file, string

constants
  className = "Lotto/getNumbers".
  classVersion = "".

class facts - displayNumbers
  leastCalledNumbers : (string LCN).
  mostCalledNumbers: (string MCN).
  oldestCalledNumbers : (string OCN).
  leastCalledRandom : (string LCR).
  randomLotto1 : (string RL1).

class predicates

  historyDataConvert : (number*, number*, number*, number*, number*,
  number*) determ (i, i, i, i, i, i).
  convertListToString : (number*, number*, string) determ (i, i, o).

clauses

  history (DisplayData):-
    existFile("LottoData.txt"),
    getHistoryData(LCN, LCMB, MCN, MCMB, OCN, OCMB, NCN, NCMB),
    historyDataConvert(LCN, LCMB, MCN, MCMB, OCN, OCMB),
    leastCalledNumbers(S1), mostCalledNumbers(S2),
    oldestCalled Numbers(S3),
    DisplayData = [S1, S2, S3],
    stdio::write("Least Called Numbers    : ", LCN, "\n"),
    stdio::write("Least Called Money Balls : ", LCMB, "\n"),
    stdio::write("Most Called Numbers     : ", MCN, "\n"),
```

## SAMPLE APPLICATION

```
        stdio::write("Most Called Money Balls   : ", MCMB, "\n"),
        stdio::write("Oldest Called Numbers     : ", OCN, "\n"),
        stdio::write("Oldest Called Money Balls: ", OCMB, "\n"),
        stdio::write("Never Called Numbers      : ", NCN, "\n"),
        stdio::write("Never Called Money Balls  : ", NCMB, "\n\n\n"), !.

    history (DisplayData):-
        existFile("LottoData.txt"),
        getHistoryDataAgain,
        getHistoryData(LCN, LCMB, MCN, MCMB, OCN, OCMB, NCN, NCMB),
        historyDataConvert(LCN, LCMB, MCN, MCMB, OCN, OCMB),
        leastCalledNumbers(S1), mostCalledNumbers(S2),
        oldestCalledNumbers(S3),
        DisplayData = [S1, S2, S3],
        stdio::write("Least Called Numbers      : ", LCN, "\n"),
        stdio::write("Least Called Money Balls  : ", LCMB, "\n"),
        stdio::write("Most Called Numbers       : ", MCN, "\n"),
        stdio::write("Most Called Money Balls   : ", MCMB, "\n"),
        stdio::write("Oldest Called Numbers     : ", OCN, "\n"),
        stdio::write("Oldest Called Money Balls: ", OCMB, "\n"),
        stdio::write("Never Called Numbers      : ", NCN, "\n"),
        stdio::write("Never Called Money Balls  : ", NCMB, "\n\n\n"), !.

    history (["", "", ""]):-
        stdio::write("Data Has Not been imported - Import data First \n\n" ),!.

    historyDataConvert(LCN, LCMB, MCN, MCMB, OCN, OCMB) :-
        convertListToString(LCN, LCMB, S1),
        convertListToString(MCN, MCMB, S2),
        convertListToString(OCN, OCMB, S3),
        assertz(leastCalledNumbers(S1)),
        assertz(mostCalledNumbers(S2)),
        assertz(oldestCalledNumbers(S3)),
        file::save(lottoNumbers, displayNumbers), !.

convertListToString([N1, N2, N3, N4, N5 | _], [MB | _], String) :-
    S1 = concat(toString(N1), ", "),
    S2 = concat(toString(N2), ", "),
    S3 = concat(toString(N3), ", "),
    S4 = concat(toString(N4), ", "),
    S5 = concat(toString(N5), " "),
    S6 = concat("- ", toString(MB)),
    String = concat(S1, S2, S3, S4, S5, S6), !.
```

```
clauses
    classInfo(className, classVersion).

end implement getNumbers
```

Please note that if you don't provide something associated with a string list in the last call to 'history()' (I provided a list of 3 empty strings), the application will compile but will bomb on execution.

Lastly, make the following modification to TaskWindow.pro. Again, due to its large size, it may be easier to get to the source code of interest by double clicking on TaskWindow.win, then click the 'code expert' button, expand the items under 'Menu' and 'Task Menu', then double click on id_get_numbers -> onGetNumbers. After you make the changes, it should look as follows:

```
predicates
    onGetNumbers : window::menuItemListener.

clauses
    onGetNumbers(_Source, _MenuTag) :-
        Form = numbers::new(This),
        Form:show(),
        getNumbers::history([L,M,O]),
        Form:set_text_from_outside_form(L), !.
```

This is where the strings are sought with 'getNumbers::history([L, M, O])', then one is placed on the form with 'Form:set_text_from _outside_form(L)'.

Make sure you save everything then rebuild the application and execute it. If you get any compiler errors, re-check all changes made. Don't worry about warnings. If all goes well you should now see the Form populated with Least Numbers Called. You can also test it by deleting all the '.txt' files except the one named 'Stats.txt' and any other ones associated with the Lotto numbers – it is up to you to track other important ones and making backups is not a bad idea.

## SAMPLE APPLICATION

If all is going well, then go ahead and do the same thing already described to place the Most Numbers Called and the Oldest Numbers Called on the Form. This will require 2 more pairs of 'Static Text' Controls on the Form. I'd place them right below the first pair and align them accordingly. Also, don't forget to make the 'Static Text" control Representation for the ones that we will change the Text for later as 'Fact Variable' as opposed to 'Variable". If you want to try something different, select both of the 'Static Text' Controls for the Least Called Numbers and do a Copy followed by a drag and drop Paste. Then go to the Properties for the new ones and make the necessary changes. However, you will notice the Control Names can not be changed and may be misleading and confusing. I recommend just creating them as you did with the first ones. As you make changes with the GUI Editor, save your changes and rebuild the application to clean the source code, but you don't have to execute right after that all the time. I'll show the source code changes below.

### Numbers.i

```
interface numbers supports formWindow
    open core

predicates
  set_form_text_for_LCN:(string).
  set_form_text_for_MCN:(string).
  set_form_text_for_OCN:(string).

end interface numbers
```

*Note: I changed the name of the other Predicate and added 2 more. The naming should help clarity a little. Changing the parameter to a string list also changes the nested implications modes to a mixture of Procedure vs Determ. That's why I just created 2 more to simplify later extensions.*

## Numbers.pro

```
clauses
  set_form_text_for_LCN(L):-
    staticText1_ctl:setText(L),
    update().                        %for eg, to repaint

  set_form_text_for_MCN(M):-
    staticText3_ctl:setText(M),
    update().                        %for eg, to repaint

  set_form_text_for_OCN(O):-
    staticText5_ctl:setText(O),
    update().                        %for eg, to repaint

facts
  again_ctl : button.
  save_ctl : button.
  staticText1_ctl : textControl.    % For Least Numbers Called
  staticText3_ctl : textControl.    % For Most Numbers Called
  staticText5_ctl : textControl.    % For Oldest Numbers Called
```

*Note: I added the comments for later referral.*

## TaskWindow.pro

```
predicates
  onGetNumbers : window::menuItemListener.

clauses
  onGetNumbers(_Source, _MenuTag) :-
    Form = numbers::new(This),
    Form:show(),
    getNumbers::history([L,M,O]),
    Form:set_form_text_for_LCN(L),
    Form:set_form_text_for_MCN(M),
    Form:set_form_text_for_OCN(O), !.
```

If everything went well, you saved all the changes, rebuilt the application and executed it; then when you select the Get Numbers Menu Option, you'll see all 3 categories on the Form. Again, if you had any compiler errors, recheck all changes made. Warnings won't hurt.

### 3.3.3.8.2 Random Numbers on the Form

Now we need to explore the part dealing with Random Numbers using history information, as well as without history (or just plain random numbers). To accommodate this, we have to remember what the range the numbers can be, as they are different for Regular Numbers (1-56) as opposed to Money Ball Numbers (1-46). Also, we want to avoid number duplications in a set. Later if you choose to explore multiple random number sets, you may wish to study options to avoid duplication of numbers in different sets (i.e. if '1' was in the first set, maybe that's the only set you want to see it in). I'll leave that exploration up to you.

Initially it would seem the existing functionality to acquire random numbers would be easier; however Prolog Domain issues can make it difficult when you start mixing domain names even though their roots are the same. Because the Domains used for the Lotto number databases are different from the ones used for the math:: random() predicate, I'll work with it as an index to a list as opposed the actual numbers themselves. I'll also do this for the Least Called Numbers category only; you can do it for the others after you see how it's done for the Least Called Numbers. This one we'll look for random numbers, if not already selected and a member of the desired history, then add them to a resultant list. The purely random ones will not look for history information. The Random Least Called Numbers will be done by randomly selecting 5 numbers that are in the Least Called Numbers data list and 1 number for the Least Called Money Balls list.

We will place all this functional source code in the GetNumbers module. The algorithms used are quite fascinating and I think you get some good exposure to some more of the PFC. To summarize

# A GUIDE TO ARTIFICIAL INTELLIGENCE WITH VISUAL PROLOG

the key algorithms, they are as follows:

The Algorithm for the Random Least Called Numbers is as follows:

```
clauses
  get_Random_LCN(LCN, LCMB):-
    N1 = tryGetNth(math::random(9), LCN),
    N2 = tryGetNth(math::random(9), LCN),
    N2 <> N1,
    N3 = tryGetNth(math::random(9), LCN),
    N3 <> N2, N3 <> N1,
    N4 = tryGetNth(math::random(9), LCN),
    N4 <> N3, N4 <> N2, N4 <> N1,
    N5 = tryGetNth(math::random(9), LCN),
    N5 <> N4, N5 <> N3, N5 <> N2, N5 <> N1,
    RandLCN = [N1, N2, N3, N4, N5],
    RandLCMB = tryGetNth(math::random(9), LCMB),
    convertListToString(RandLCN, [RandLCMB], S),
    assert(leastCalledRandom(S)), !.
  get_Random_LCN(LCN, LCMB):- get_Random_LCN(LCN, LCMB).
```

*Note: It gets the 2 lists of Least Called Numbers and Least Called Money Balls. The tryGetNth() predicate is part of the PFC List functionality.*

The Algorithm for just the Random Numbers is as follows:

```
clauses
  get_Random():-
    assert(regularNumbers([ 1, 2, 3, 4, 5, 6, 7, 8, 9,10,11,12,13,14,
                15,16,17,18,19,20, 21,22,23,24,25,26,
                27,28,29,30,31,32,33,34,35,36,37,38,39,
                40, 41,42,43,44,45,46,47,48,49,50,51,
                52,53,54,55,56])),
    assert(moneyBallNumbers([ 1, 2, 3, 4, 5, 6, 7, 8, 9,10,11,12,13,14,
                15,16,17,18,19,20,21,22,23,24, 25,26,
                27,28,29,30,31,32,33,34,35,36,37,38,
                39,40,41,42,43,44,45,46])),
    regularNumbers(Ns),
    moneyBallNumbers(MBs),
```

```
        N1 = tryGetNth(math::random(55)+1, Ns),
        N2 = tryGetNth(math::random(55)+1, Ns),
        N2 <> N1,
        N3 = tryGetNth(math::random(55)+1, Ns),
        N3 <> N2, N3 <> N1,
        N4 = tryGetNth(math::random(55)+1, Ns),
        N4 <> N3, N4 <> N2, N4 <> N1,
        N5 = tryGetNth(math::random(55)+1, Ns),
        N5 <> N4, N5 <> N3, N5 <> N2, N5 <> N1,
        RN = [N1, N2, N3, N4, N5],
        RMB = [tryGetNth(math::random(45)+1, MBs)],
        convertListToString(RN, RMB, S),
        assert(randomLotto1(S)),
        retract(regularNumbers(_)),
        retract(moneyBallNumbers(_)), !.
    get_Random():- get_Random().
```

*Note: Keep in mind random numbers start at 0.*

So for complete changes for all the modules and form to accommodate the Random Least Called Numbers and the Random Numbers, the details are as follows:

**Numbers.frm (Form)**

Using the Form GUI Editor, add 4 more 'Static Text' Controls (or 2 pair) as done previously. The left side ones should have the Properties Text changed to 'Random Least Called: " and 'Random1 : ". Don't forget to change the right hand side Representations to 'Fact Variable'

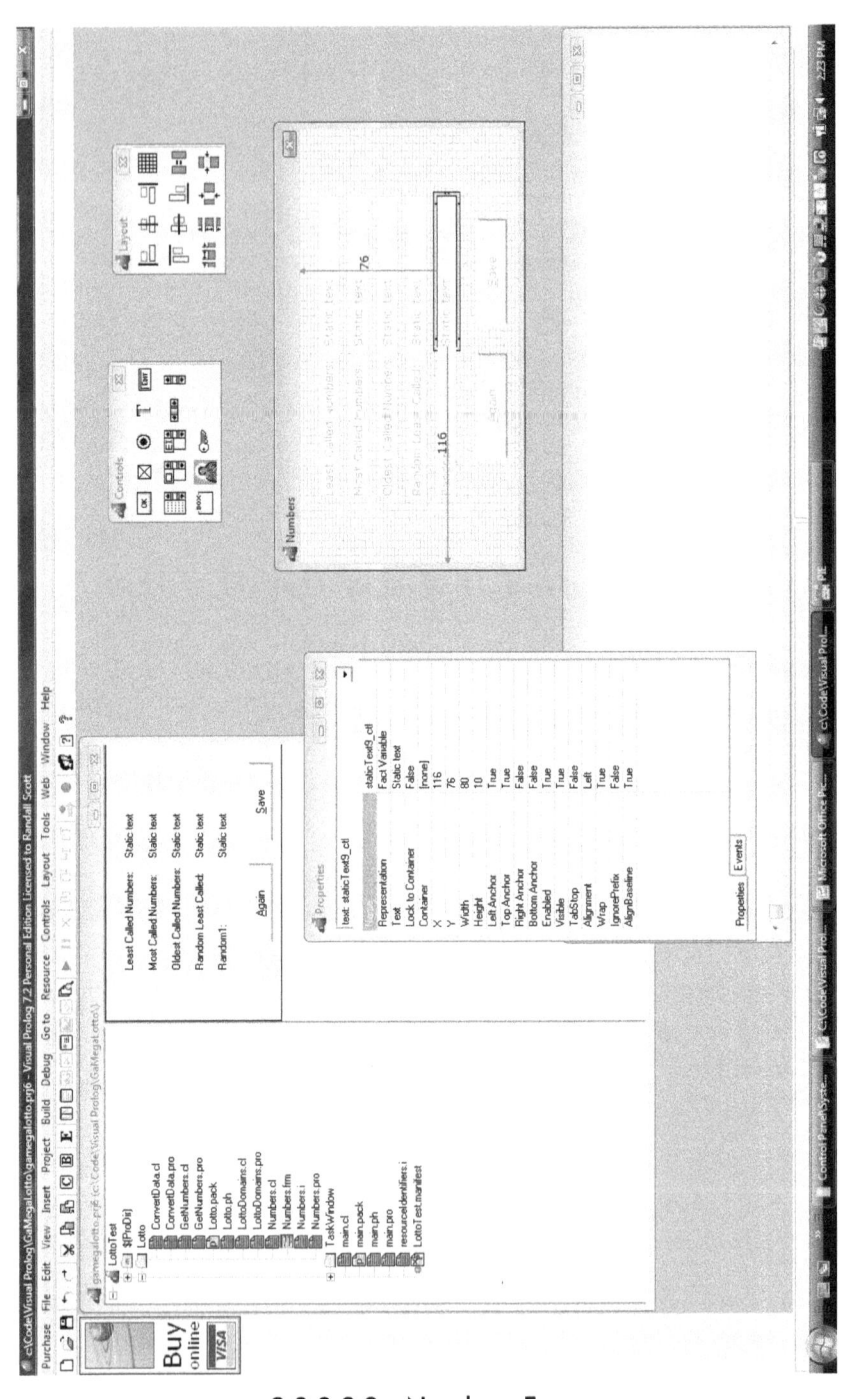

## A GUIDE TO ARTIFICIAL INTELLIGENCE WITH VISUAL PROLOG

**3.3.3.8.2 - Numbers Form**

102

## Numbers.i (Form Interface)

```
interface numbers supports formWindow
   open core

predicates
   set_form_text_for_LCN:(string).
   set_form_text_for_MCN:(string).
   set_form_text_for_OCN:(string).
   set_form_text_for_RLCN:(string).
   set_form_text_for_RAN:(string).

end interface numbers
```

*Note: Two more lines to fill in the random numbers on the form.*

## Numbers.pro (Form Implementation abstract)

```
clauses
   set_form_text_for_LCN(L):-
      staticText1_ctl:setText(L),
      update().                        % to repaint
   set_form_text_for_MCN(M):-
      staticText3_ctl:setText(M),
      update().                        % to repaint

   set_form_text_for_OCN(O):-
      staticText5_ctl:setText(O),
      update().                        % to repaint

   set_form_text_for_RLCN(RLCN):-
      staticText7_ctl:setText(RLCN),
      update().                        % to repaint

   set_form_text_for_RAN(R):-
      staticText9_ctl:setText(R),
      update().                        % to repaint
facts
   again_ctl : button.
   save_ctl : button.
   staticText1_ctl : textControl.      % For Least Called Numbers
```

```
staticText3_ctl : textControl.        % For Most Called Numbers
staticText5_ctl : textControl.        % For Oldest Called Numbers
staticText7_ctl : textControl.        % For Random LCN
staticText9_ctl : textControl.        % For Random Numbers
```

## GetNumbers.cl (for visible Predicate declarations)

```
class getNumbers
    open core, lottoDomains, convertData

predicates
    history : (string*) procedure ([o, o, o, o, o]).

    classInfo : core::classInfo.
    % @short Class information predicate.
    % @detail This predicate represents information predicate of this class.
    % @end

end class getNumbers
```

Note: Two more strings added to the 'history()' parameters. You could just drop the list brackets on the flow and list it as a single 'o'. However, I like this approach to remind you its set for only 5 elements of a list.

## GetNumbers.pro (module Implementation)

```
implement getNumbers
    open core, lottoDomains, convertData, file, string, list

constants
    className = "Lotto/getNumbers".
    classVersion = "".

class facts - displayNumbers
    leastCalledNumbers : (string LCN).
    mostCalledNumbers: (string MCN).
    oldestCalledNumbers : (string OCN).
    leastCalledRandom : (string LCR).
    randomLotto1 : (string RL1).
```

## SAMPLE APPLICATION

```
class facts - tempLocal
   regularNumbers     : (number* RN).
   moneyBallNumbers : (number* MBN).

class predicates

   historyDataConvert : (number*, number*, number*, number*, number*,
   number*) determ (i, i, i, i, i, i).
   convertListToString : (number*, number*, string) determ (i, i, o).
   get_Random_LCN : (number*, number*).
   get_Random : ().

clauses

   history (DisplayData):-
      existFile("LottoData.txt"),
      getHistoryData(LCN, LCMB, MCN, MCMB, OCN, OCMB, NCN, NCMB),
      historyDataConvert(LCN, LCMB, MCN, MCMB, OCN, OCMB),
      get_Random_LCN(LCN, LCMB),
      get_Random(),
      leastCalledNumbers(S1),
      mostCalledNumbers(S2),
      oldestCalledNumbers(S3),
      leastCalledRandom(S4),
      randomLotto1(S5),
      DisplayData = [S1, S2, S3, S4, S5],
      stdio::write("Least Called Numbers     : ", LCN, "\n"),
      stdio::write("Least Called Money Balls : ", LCMB, "\n"),
      stdio::write("Most Called Numbers      : ", MCN, "\n"),
      stdio::write("Most Called Money Balls  : ", MCMB, "\n"),
      stdio::write("Oldest Called Numbers    : ", OCN, "\n"),
      stdio::write("Oldest Called Money Balls: ", OCMB, "\n"),
      stdio::write("Never Called Numbers     : ", NCN, "\n"),
      stdio::write("Never Called Money Balls : ", NCMB, "\n\n\n"), !.

   history (DisplayData):-
      existFile("LottoData.txt"),
      getHistoryDataAgain,
      getHistoryData(LCN, LCMB, MCN, MCMB, OCN, OCMB, NCN, NCMB),
      historyDataConvert(LCN, LCMB, MCN, MCMB, OCN, OCMB),
      get_Random_LCN(LCN, LCMB),
      get_Random(),
      leastCalledNumbers(S1),
      mostCalledNumbers(S2),
```

### A GUIDE TO ARTIFICIAL INTELLIGENCE WITH VISUAL PROLOG

```
        oldestCalledNumbers(S3),
        leastCalledRandom(S4),
        randomLotto1(S5),
        DisplayData = [S1, S2, S3, S4, S5],
        stdio::write("Least Called Numbers      : ", LCN, "\n"),
        stdio::write("Least Called Money Balls : ", LCMB, "\n"),
        stdio::write("Most Called Numbers       : ", MCN, "\n"),
        stdio::write("Most Called Money Balls   : ", MCMB, "\n"),
        stdio::write("Oldest Called Numbers     : ", OCN, "\n"),
        stdio::write("Oldest Called Money Balls: ", OCMB, "\n"),
        stdio::write("Never Called Numbers      : ", NCN, "\n"),
        stdio::write("Never Called Money Balls : ", NCMB, "\n\n\n"), !.

    history (["","","","",""]):-
        stdio::write("Data Has Not been imported - Import data First \n\n" ),!.

    get_Random_LCN(LCN, LCMB):-
        N1 = tryGetNth(math::random(9), LCN),
        N2 = tryGetNth(math::random(9), LCN),
        N2 <> N1,
        N3 = tryGetNth(math::random(9), LCN),
        N3 <> N2, N3 <> N1,
        N4 = tryGetNth(math::random(9), LCN),
        N4 <> N3, N4 <> N2, N4 <> N1,
        N5 = tryGetNth(math::random(9), LCN),
        N5 <> N4, N5 <> N3, N5 <> N2, N5 <> N1,
        RandLCN = [N1, N2, N3, N4, N5],
        RandLCMB = tryGetNth(math::random(9), LCMB),
        convertListToString(RandLCN, [RandLCMB], S),
        assert(leastCalledRandom(S)), !.
    get_Random_LCN(LCN, LCMB):- get_Random_LCN(LCN, LCMB).

    get_Random():-
        assert(regularNumbers([ 1, 2, 3, 4, 5, 6, 7, 8, 9,10,11,12,13, 14,
                        15,16,17,18,19,20, 21,22,23,24,25,26,
                        27, 28,29,30,31,32,33,34,35,36,37,38,
                        39,40, 41,42,43,44,45,46,47,48,49,50,
                        51,52,53,54,55,56])),
        assert(moneyBallNumbers([ 1, 2, 3, 4, 5, 6, 7, 8, 9,10,11,12,13,
                        14,15, 16,17,18,19,20,21,22,23,24,
                        25,26,27,28,  29, 30,31,32,33,34,35,
                        36,37,38,39,40,41, 42,43,44,45,46])),
        regularNumbers(Ns),
        moneyBallNumbers(MBs),
```

## SAMPLE APPLICATION

```
            N1 = tryGetNth(math::random(55)+1, Ns),
            N2 = tryGetNth(math::random(55)+1, Ns),
            N2 <> N1,
            N3 = tryGetNth(math::random(55)+1, Ns),
            N3 <> N2, N3 <> N1,
            N4 = tryGetNth(math::random(55)+1, Ns),
            N4 <> N3, N4 <> N2, N4 <> N1,
            N5 = tryGetNth(math::random(55)+1, Ns),
            N5 <> N4, N5 <> N3, N5 <> N2, N5 <> N1,
            RN = [N1, N2, N3, N4, N5],
            RMB = [tryGetNth(math::random(45)+1, MBs)],
            convertListToString(RN, RMB, S),
            assert(randomLotto1(S)),
            retract(regularNumbers(_)),
            retract(moneyBallNumbers(_)), !.
        get_Random():- get_Random().

    historyDataConvert(LCN, LCMB, MCN, MCMB, OCN, OCMB) :-
        convertListToString(LCN, LCMB, S1),
        convertListToString(MCN, MCMB, S2),
        convertListToString(OCN, OCMB, S3),
        assertz(leastCalledNumbers(S1)),
        assertz(mostCalledNumbers(S2)),
        assertz(oldestCalledNumbers(S3)),
        file::save(lottoNumbers, displayNumbers), !.

    convertListToString([N1, N2, N3, N4, N5 | _], [MB | _], String) :-
        S1 = concat(toString(N1), ", "),
        S2 = concat(toString(N2), ", "),
        S3 = concat(toString(N3), ", "),
        S4 = concat(toString(N4), ", "),
        S5 = concat(toString(N5), " "),
        S6 = concat("- ", toString(MB)),
        String = concat(S1, S2, S3, S4, S5, S6), !.

clauses
    classInfo(className, classVersion).

end implement getNumbers
```

Note: **list** was added to the open statement and another local database was added.

## TaskWindow.pro

```
predicates
  onGetNumbers : window::menuItemListener.

clauses
  onGetNumbers(_Source, _MenuTag) :-
    Form = numbers::new(This),
    Form:show(),
    getNumbers::history([L, M, O, RL, R]),
    Form:set_form_text_for_LCN(L),
    Form:set_form_text_for_MCN(M),
    Form:set_form_text_for_OCN(O),
    Form:set_form_text_for_RLCN(RL),
    Form:set_form_text_for_RAN(R), !.
```

*Note: Don't forget to more easily access this code in the TaskWindow.pro, do it through TaskWindow.win, Code Expert, and the Menu Tree.*

Go ahead and rebuild and execute to see results. Again, if you have any compiler errors check all spelling. Warnings are OK. The Form should now show all the numbers we were looking for in the format we designed.

### 3.3.3.8.3 Form Buttons

So far we can display what we want; however, we can't redo the random number options or save them for later print options. That is why we kept two of the buttons. Our Form has 2 buttons we renamed to get Random numbers repeatedly until you see some you like; as well as one to save the numbers displayed for printing out. These Buttons were labeled 'Again' and 'Save'. The "Save" one should be easiest, as we will use the file save predicate to save the consultable database ('displayNumbers') we created, that conveniently has the names of the categories as data element names that are descriptive of the numbers we're interested in. This will be activated by the form *event* of the Button Click.

## SAMPLE APPLICATION

Go to the Form GUI Editor and double click on Numbers.frm in the Project Tree. Click on the 'Save' Button to select it. Then go to the Properties Dialog Box, and at the bottom of it click on 'Events' tab (as opposed to 'Properties'). The event we're interested in is 'ClickResponder'. To the right of it, click the down arrow and select 'OnSaveClick'. Exit the GUI Editor and save your changes. Also rebuild the application to effect source code associated with the GUI Editor changes. Now enter the Form Implementation (Numbers.pro) and look for the *predicates* and *clauses* section for the 'onSaveClick' predicate declaration and definitions. We will tie some code here; however, most of our implementation parts will be in the 'GetNumbers' module, which we will work with first.

To do this we'll need a visible Predicate in GetNumbers to save the file, which we'll call from the 'onSaveClick.' clause. We'll call it 'saveHistory' and place it in GetNumbers.cl. Then we can create the implementation part in GetNumbers.pro using the following call:

```
saveHistory():-
  file::existFile(lottoNumbers),
  file::delete(lottoNumbers),
  file::save(lottoNumbers, displayNumbers),
  retract(leastCalledNumbers(_)),
  retract(mostCalledNumbers(_)),
  retract(oldestCalledNumbers(_)),
  retract(leastCalledRandom(_)),
  retract(randomLotto1(_)),!.

saveHistory():-
  file::save(lottoNumbers, displayNumbers),
  retract(leastCalledNumbers(_)),
  retract(mostCalledNumbers(_)),
  retract(oldestCalledNumbers(_)),
  retract(leastCalledRandom(_)),
  retract(randomLotto1(_)),!.

saveHistory():- !.
```

Every time you click on 'Save', the data gets saved and the form goes away. However, there is no need to keep the data resident in the local database, which is why it is retracted. The last 'saveHistory()' was placed to avoid the shift from 'procedure' mode to 'determ' mode (i.e. removed all possibilities of failure). Now we can go back to the 'Numbers.pro' to make the call to 'saveHistory'. The changes that need to be made should look as follows:

```
predicates
    onSaveClick : button::clickResponder.

clauses
    onSaveClick(_Source) = button::defaultAction:-
        getNumbers::saveHistory().
```

As for the 'Again' Button we need to do something somewhat similar to 'Save' Button in setting the Event for 'onAgainClick'. However, our functionality is intended to redo the Random Numbers displayed. Also, we need to change the action taken after the click so the Form doesn't close like it will when we click on the 'Save' Button. Again, we need a visible Predicate in GetNumbers.cl to do this so, we'll create a new one and name it 'randomAgain'. The functionality for the 'Again' button is going to get somewhat complex, because we want to avoid randomly selecting numbers and getting duplicates in the final sets for both categories. There are probably many different approaches to accomplish this, however the approach I'm taking (as explained earlier) helps mitigate some of the challenges Prolog presents when mixing your declared domains with those already built in Visual Prolog, as well with those in the PFC. If you find a better approach please help yourself; however, you should be able to follow along with the approach I took. I'll list all the source code changes first, then try to elaborate a little on some of the rationale.

## GetNumbers.cl

```
class getNumbers
    open core, lottoDomains, convertData
```

## SAMPLE APPLICATION

predicates

```
history : (string*) procedure ([o, o, o, o, o]).
saveHistory : ().
randomAgain : (string, string) procedure (o, o).

classInfo : core::classInfo.
% @short Class information  predicate.
% @detail This predicate represents information predicate of this class.
% @end
```

end class getNumbers

# GetNumber.pro

```
implement getNumbers
    open core, lottoDomains, convertData, file, string, math, list

constants
    className = "Lotto/getNumbers".
    classVersion = "".

class facts - displayNumbers
    leastCalledNumbers : (string LCN).
    mostCalledNumbers: (string MCN).
    oldestCalledNumbers : (string OCN).
    leastCalledRandom : (string LCR).
    randomLotto1 : (string RL1).

class facts - tempLocal
    regularNumbers    : (number* RN).
    moneyBallNumbers : (number* MBN).

class predicates

    historyDataConvert : (number*, number*, number*, number*, number*,
     number*) determ (i, i, i, i, i).
    convertListToString : (number*, number*, string) determ (i, i, o).
    get_Random_LCN : (number*, number*).
    get_Random : ().

clauses
```

## A GUIDE TO ARTIFICIAL INTELLIGENCE WITH VISUAL PROLOG

```
history (DisplayData):-
    existFile("LottoData.txt"),
    getHistoryData(LCN, LCMB, MCN, MCMB, OCN, OCMB, NCN, NCMB),
    historyDataConvert(LCN, LCMB, MCN, MCMB, OCN, OCMB),
    get_Random_LCN(LCN, LCMB),
    get_Random(),
    leastCalledNumbers(S1),
    mostCalledNumbers(S2),
    oldestCalledNumbers(S3),
    leastCalledRandom(S4),
    randomLotto1(S5),
    DisplayData = [S1, S2, S3, S4, S5],
    stdio::write("Least Called Numbers     : ", LCN, "\n"),
    stdio::write("Least Called Money Balls : ", LCMB, "\n"),
    stdio::write("Most Called Numbers      : ", MCN, "\n"),
    stdio::write("Most Called Money Balls  : ", MCMB, "\n"),
    stdio::write("Oldest Called Numbers    : ", OCN, "\n"),
    stdio::write("Oldest Called Money Balls: ", OCMB, "\n"),
    stdio::write("Never Called Numbers     : ", NCN, "\n"),
    stdio::write("Never Called Money Balls : ", NCMB, "\n\n\n"), !.

history (DisplayData):-
    existFile("LottoData.txt"),
    getHistoryDataAgain,
    getHistoryData(LCN, LCMB, MCN, MCMB, OCN, OCMB, NCN, NCMB),
    historyDataConvert(LCN, LCMB, MCN, MCMB, OCN, OCMB),
    get_Random_LCN(LCN, LCMB),
    get_Random(),
    leastCalledNumbers(S1),
    mostCalledNumbers(S2),
    oldestCalledNumbers(S3),
    leastCalledRandom(S4),
    randomLotto1(S5),
    DisplayData = [S1, S2, S3, S4, S5],
    stdio::write("Least Called Numbers     : ", LCN, "\n"),
    stdio::write("Least Called Money Balls : ", LCMB, "\n"),
    stdio::write("Most Called Numbers      : ", MCN, "\n"),
    stdio::write("Most Called Money Balls  : ", MCMB, "\n"),
    stdio::write("Oldest Called Numbers    : ", OCN, "\n"),
    stdio::write("Oldest Called Money Balls: ", OCMB, "\n"),
    stdio::write("Never Called Numbers     : ", NCN, "\n"),
    stdio::write("Never Called Money Balls : ", NCMB, "\n\n\n"), !.
```

## SAMPLE APPLICATION

```
history (["", "","","", ""]):-
   stdio::write("Data Has Not been imported - Import data First \n\n" ),!.

get_Random_LCN(LCN, LCMB):-
   N1 = tryGetNth(math::random(9), LCN),
   N2 = tryGetNth(math::random(9), LCN),
   N2 <> N1,
   N3 = tryGetNth(math::random(9), LCN),
   N3 <> N2, N3 <> N1,
   N4 = tryGetNth(math::random(9), LCN),
   N4 <> N3, N4 <> N2, N4 <> N1,
   N5 = tryGetNth(math::random(9), LCN),
   N5 <> N4, N5 <> N3, N5 <> N2, N5 <> N1,
   RandLCN = [N1, N2, N3, N4, N5],
   RandLCMB = tryGetNth(math::random(9), LCMB),
   convertListToString(RandLCN, [RandLCMB], S),
   assert(leastCalledRandom(S)), !.
get_Random_LCN(LCN, LCMB):- get_Random_LCN(LCN, LCMB).

get_Random():-
   assert(regularNumbers([ 1, 2, 3, 4, 5, 6, 7, 8, 9,10,11,12,13,14,
                    15,16,17,18,19,20,21,22,23,24,25, 26,
                    27, 28,29,30,31,32,33,34,35,36,37,38,
                    39,40, 41,42,43,44,45,46,47,48,49,50,
                    51,52,53,54,55,56])),
   assert(moneyBallNumbers([ 1, 2, 3, 4, 5, 6, 7, 8, 9,10,11,12,13,
                    14,15,16,17,18,19,20, 21,22,23,24,25,
                    26,27,28,29,30,31,32,33,34,35,36,37,
                    38,39,40,41,42,43,44,45,46])),
   regularNumbers(Ns),
   moneyBallNumbers(MBs),
   N1 = tryGetNth(math::random(55)+1, Ns),
   N2 = tryGetNth(math::random(55)+1, Ns),
   N2 <> N1,
   N3 = tryGetNth(math::random(55)+1, Ns),
   N3 <> N2, N3 <> N1,
   N4 = tryGetNth(math::random(55)+1, Ns),
   N4 <> N3, N4 <> N2, N4 <> N1,
   N5 = tryGetNth(math::random(55)+1, Ns),
   N5 <> N4, N5 <> N3, N5 <> N2, N5 <> N1,
   RN = [N1, N2, N3, N4, N5],
   RMB = [tryGetNth(math::random(45)+1, MBs)],
   convertListToString(RN, RMB, S),
   assert(randomLotto1(S)),
```

## A GUIDE TO ARTIFICIAL INTELLIGENCE WITH VISUAL PROLOG

```
    retract(regularNumbers(_)),
    retract(moneyBallNumbers(_)), !.
get_Random():- get_Random().

randomAgain(RL, R):-
    retract(leastCalledRandom(_)),
    retract(randomLotto1(_)),
    getHistoryData(LCN, LCMB, _, _, _, _, _, _),
    get_Random_LCN(LCN, LCMB),
    get_Random(),
    leastCalledRandom(RL),
    randomLotto1(R),!.
randomAgain("", "") :- !.

historyDataConvert(LCN, LCMB, MCN, MCMB, OCN, OCMB) :-
    convertListToString(LCN, LCMB, S1),
    convertListToString(MCN, MCMB, S2),
    convertListToString(OCN, OCMB, S3),
    assertz(leastCalledNumbers(S1)),
    assertz(mostCalledNumbers(S2)),
    assertz(oldestCalledNumbers(S3)),
    file::save(lottoNumbers, displayNumbers), !.

convertListToString([N1, N2, N3, N4, N5 | _], [MB | _], String) :-
    S1 = concat(toString(N1), ", "),
    S2 = concat(toString(N2), ", "),
    S3 = concat(toString(N3), ", "),
    S4 = concat(toString(N4), ", "),
    S5 = concat(toString(N5), " "),
    S6 = concat("- ", toString(MB)),
    String = concat(S1, S2, S3, S4, S5, S6), !.

saveHistory():-
    file::existFile(lottoNumbers),
    file::delete(lottoNumbers),
    file::save(lottoNumbers, displayNumbers),
    retract(leastCalledNumbers(_)),
    retract(mostCalledNumbers(_)),
    retract(oldestCalledNumbers(_)),
    retract(leastCalledRandom(_)),
    retract(randomLotto1(_)),!.

saveHistory():-
    file::save(lottoNumbers, displayNumbers),
```

```
        retract(leastCalledNumbers(_)),
        retract(mostCalledNumbers(_)),
        retract(oldestCalledNumbers(_)),
        retract(leastCalledRandom(_)),
        retract(randomLotto1(_)),!.

    saveHistory():- !.

clauses
    classInfo(className, classVersion).

end implement getNumbers
```

## Numbers.pro (abstract)

```
    predicates
      onSaveClick : button::clickResponder.

    clauses
      onSaveClick(_Source) = button::defaultAction:-
        getNumbers::saveHistory().

    predicates
      onAgainClick : button::clickResponder.

    clauses
      onAgainClick(_Source) = button::noAction :-
        getNumbers::randomAgain(RL, R),
        staticText7_ctl:setText(RL),
        staticText9_ctl:setText(R),
        update().

% This code is maintained automatically, do not update it manually.
20:10:44-16.7.2009
facts
    again_ctl : button.
    save_ctl : button.
    staticText1_ctl : textControl.    % For Least Called Numbers
    staticText3_ctl : textControl.    % For Most Called Numbers
    staticText5_ctl : textControl.    % For Oldest Called Numbers
    staticText7_ctl : textControl.    % For Random LCN
    staticText9_ctl : textControl.    % For Random Numbers
```

You should notice the 'Save' button uses the 'defaultAction' which will cause the Form to close when clicked as well, so I changed it to 'noAction' for the 'Again' Button. I also chose not to comment out or remove the messages sent to the Message Window so you could evaluate the random numbers selected from the Least Called Numbers, as well as the pure random ones. Go ahead rebuild and execute the application. Again, if you get any errors recheck all your work.

### 3.3.3.8.4 Form Summary

That pretty much completes the challenges of getting Lottery History information and Random Numbers for 2 categories, then displaying them on a Form. You were given a somewhat wide exposure to some of the PFC functionality used with the form. I also tried to give you some exposure to some of the predicate *modes* available. However, there is a lot more Eye Candy issues you should explore with Forms and Windows, now that you know how to access Objects as well as their Methods. Some of these involve changing fonts (style, size, color, and other attributes), Form background and foreground colors, as well as using many of the other Control Tools available. This should be enough to get you started with just about any application. The more you explore, the more programming gifts you will acquire.

### 3.3.3.8.5 Printing the Numbers

Print options will depend on if you are using the Personal Version vs. the Commercial Version. For the Personal Version, the easiest approach would be to just write the information out to a file formatting the Data as you wish, then use Microsoft Notepad or some Word Processor application to print it out. The Commercial Version has much better Print Options from within your source code. The Personal Edition does not provide any easy method for sending information to a Printer, so I chose to just leave it out; and, you can

## SAMPLE APPLICATION

use Microsoft Notepad or some kind of Word Processing application to open the file we saved as 'LottoNumbers.txt' and print it from there. If you want your application to do it directly and fairly easily, then I suggest you procure the Commercial Edition.

### 3.3.3.8.6 Providing Help

As for the Help feature, either create a Text Object with the '.txt' filename extension or create a Text file with Microsoft Notepad (with the '.txt' filename extension); and populate it with the instructions you wish to provide your target user. I think explaining how to download and massage the Lottery information for importation would be good help. Then make it viewable when selected from the Menu Help option. How to make it viewable can be quite fascinating – I'll start by making it viewable in the Message Window.

In the Reference Section you will also find the Information I will be providing for the Import Procedure Instructions; you may wish to explore and modify as necessary when providing help from the Menu. You could use whatever name you wish; but, for simplicity I named it 'ImportInstructions.hlp'. Create this file and save it with the 'Stats.txt' file in the 'Exe' folder of this project. Microsoft won't like the filename extension because it uses this same one for other files formatted differently, for its somewhat generic way of dealing with Help. However, your Lotto application will not have any problem reading it. Keep in mind if you are re-doing this application as this book describes, at several locations I instruct you to delete all '.txt' files except the one named 'Stats.txt'. If we named this one with the '.txt' extension, it may accidentally get deleted. The way I created it, was to create it in Microsoft Notepad and saved it as 'ImportInstructions.txt', then using Microsoft Explorer I renamed it to 'ImportInstructions.hlp'.

Don't forget to activate the Menu Item as well using the 'TaskMenu.mnu' Menu GUI Editor – you might want to check the activation marks for 'Help' itself, as well as both submenu items. For simplicity, initially when you use the Help menu item for Download

### A GUIDE TO ARTIFICIAL INTELLIGENCE WITH VISUAL PROLOG

Instructions, I send it to the Message Window. Later on, we will explore other options.

In addition, you may want to use the Dialog GUI Editor as well to modify the 'AboutDialog.dlg' to be a little more descriptive of this application when selected from the 'Help' menu. It will already have 4 Static Text controls, of which you can change the Text with the Properties dialog box. Most of the 'About' changes can be accomplished using the Properties Window while in the Dialog GUI Editor.

Note: I could have used an algorithm similar to the one I used to read the 'Stats.txt' file one line at a time and send it to the Message Window one line at a time. However, if you take the time to analize a lot of the functionality that comes with Visual Prolog in the PFC, you will find a more elegant solution with a predicate that come with 'file'. See below:

### Similar Algorithm used to read Stats.txt

```
displayHelp():-
    stdio::write("\n\nData Import and Massaging Instructions\n\n"),
    I = inputStream_file::openFile8(lottoHelpFile),
    getHelp(I), !.

getHelp(I) :-
        not(I:endOfStream()),
        InstructionLine = I:readLine(),
        stdio::write(InstructionLine, "\n"),
        getHelp(I).
getHelp(_):-!.
```

With predicate declaration getHelp : ( inputstream)

### Better approach

```
displayHelp():-
    HelpStr = file::readString(lottoHelpFile, Boolean),
    Help = concat("-------------Data Import and Massaging Instructions-----
-----------\n\n", HelpStr),
    stdio::write(Help), !.
```

Abstracts of the added Help Menu source code is as follows:

## GetNumbers.cl (abstract)

```
predicates
  history : (string*)  procedure ([o, o, o, o, o]).
  saveHistory : ().
  randomAgain : (string, string) procedure (o, o).
  displayHelp : ().
```

## GetNumbers.pro (abstract)

```
class predicates
  historyDataConvert : (number*, number*, number*, number*, number*,
  number*) determ (i, i, i, i, i, i).
  convertListToString : (number*, number*, string) determ (i, i, o).
  get_Random_LCN : (number*, number*) multi (i, i).
  get_Random : ().

clauses
  displayHelp():-
    HelpStr = file::readString(lottoHelpFile, Boolean),
    Help = concat(
    "---------------Data Import and Massaging Instructions-----------------\n\n",
    HelpStr),
    stdio::write(Help), !.
```

## TaskWindow.pro (abstract)

```
predicates
  onHelpDownloadProcedure : window::menuItemListener.

clauses
  onHelpDownloadProcedure(_Source, _MenuTag):-
    getNumbers::displayHelp.
```

*Note: Make sure the menu options for Help are activated.*

OK, this works as intended; however, this information gets displayed as mixed with other information that gets sent to the

Message Window as well. To see it all, you have to scroll up and down and find where it starts. It may be necessary to clear the window before selecting the Help menu item. I think it would be better to send this Help information to a Form or separate Window; and for this purpose I will first try sending it to a Form Object as well to compare and contrast positives and negatives of the approach.

Go ahead and create a form object similar to how you created one for Numbers and give it the name of 'Help'. We won't need any buttons, so you can delete all of them. You will need to make the Form quite large in hopes of filling it with the Help Information you previously sent to the Message Window. In the proprties you can set the VertScrollBar option to true. Next place a Static Text Control on it similar to how you did it for Numbers. In this case, all you will need is just one Text Control. Resize it and make it fill the Form as much as possible. Don't forget to make it a Fact Variable. The only challenge next is to send the Help String to the Static Text Control of the 'Help' Form. So we will need to change the 'displayHelp()' predicate to have one output parameter which will return the 'HelpStr' string so we can put it in the Text Control of the Form through the Task Window Help menu listener. This will require a few lines of code to be added to the TaskWindow.pro file. Abstracts of the changes are as follows:

## GetNumbers.cl (abstract)

```
predicates
    history : (string*)  procedure ([o, o, o, o, o]).
    saveHistory : ().
    randomAgain : (string, string) procedure (o, o).
    displayHelp : (string) procedure (o).
```

## GetNumbers.pro (abstract)

```
clauses
    displayHelp(Help):-
        HelpStr = file::readString(lottoHelpFile, IsUnicode),
```

## SAMPLE APPLICATION

```
        Help = concat(
        "---------------Data Import and Massaging Instructions-----------------\n\n",
        HelpStr),
        stdio::write(Help), !.
```

## Help.i

```
    interface help supports formWindow
      open core

    predicates
      set_form_text:(string).

    end interface help
```

## Help.pro (Abstract)

```
    implement help
      inherits formWindow
      open core, vpiDomains

    constants
      className = "Lotto/help".
      classVersion = "".

    clauses
      classInfo(className, classVersion).

    clauses
      display(Parent) = Form :-
        Form = new(Parent),
        Form.show().

    clauses
      new(Parent):-
        formWindow::new(Parent),
        generatedInitialize().

    clauses
      set_form_text(Help):-
        staticText_ctl:setForegroundColor(color_Blue ),
        staticText_ctl:setText(Help),
```

```
    update().                %to repaint
% This code is maintained automatically, do not update it manually.
% 12:58:50-11.8.2009
facts
    staticText_ctl : textControl.
```

## TaskWindow.pro (Abstract)

```
predicates
    onHelpDownloadProcedure : window::menuItemListener.
clauses
    onHelpDownloadProcedure(_Source, _MenuTag):-
        Form2 = help::new(This),
        Form2:show(),
        getNumbers::displayHelp(Help),
        Form2:set_form_text(Help),!.
```

If you noticed above, with a little research you can provide a way of changing the font color through the 'setForegroundColor()' method. However, I could not find a way to change the background color to something other than gray - maybe it is out there somewhere and I just haven't found it yet. Ok, this works a little different than sending it to the Message Window; however, in order to see it all, you need to maximize the Task Window, which is it's parent. This was interesting, but I would prefer to just send it to a simple Window (no Menus or Toolbars) with a white background and a black font color, and with scroll options if the window is small.

This is where I think I will take you one step beyond the Modules you created and Objects that Visual Prolog creates; and, demonstrate for you how to create a Window Object. Actually, Visual Prolog previously provided this option in an earlier version which you could select from the Project items like forms, menus, toolbars, etc. However, I'm sure it was removed for good reasons.

When you create this Window object you will not create a '.win' resource file or have the luxury of a Window GUI Editor for accessing some its properties like you do for TaskWindow. win. However, I think it is important you appreciate the vastness of features that are embodied in Visual Prolog; and, with a little study and experimentation you can and will go through an amazing discovery process — I know I have and continue to do so. I found a lot of great assisting information from the Example 'Editor' and available Personal Edition PFC structure (Commercial Edition has a lot more) for this window creation effort.

To Create our Help Window Object, you will create another Class (not a module this time) and give it the name of 'HelpWindow'. Remember to use 'add new in existing' and place it in our package folder for Lotto. Before you click on the Create Button, make sure the 'Create Objects' check mark is checked, select 'Existing Interface', then select 'window' for the 'Existing Interface'.

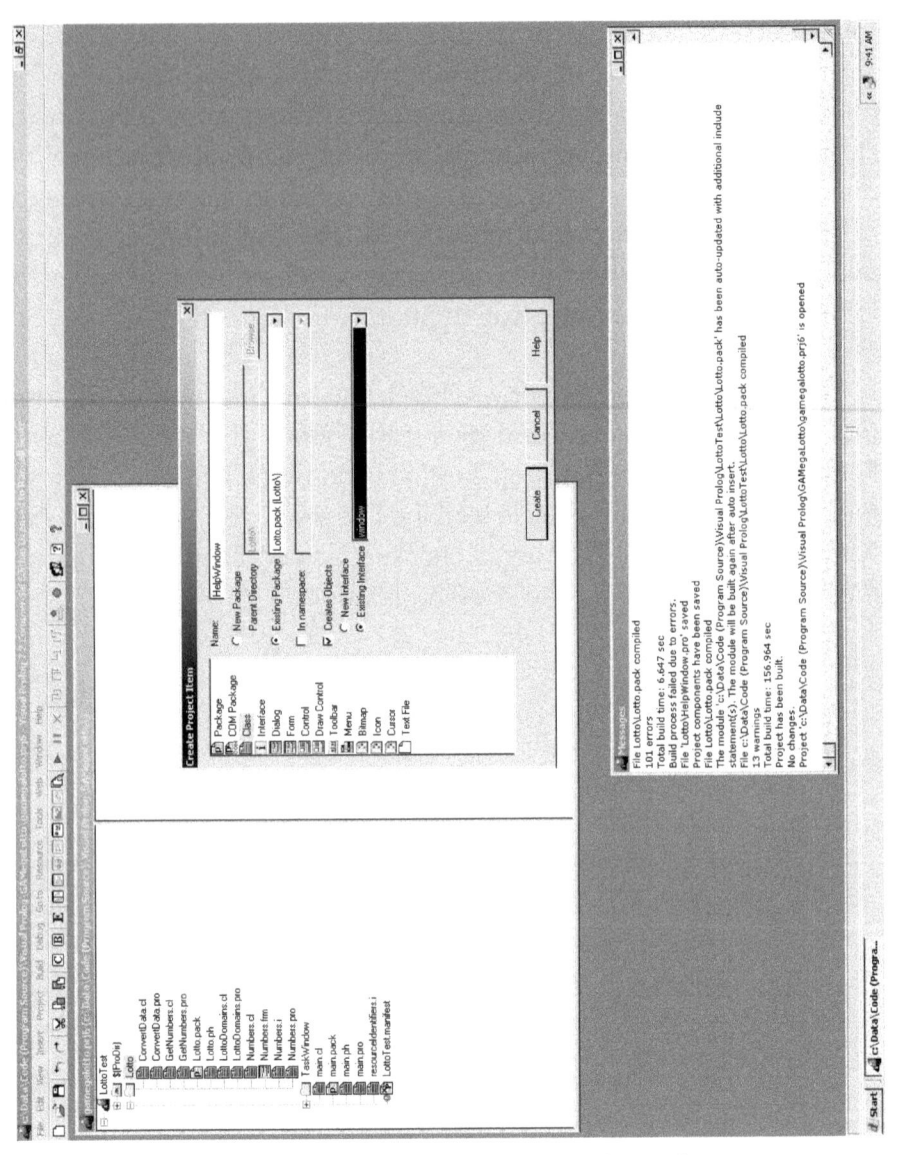

◄ A GUIDE TO ARTIFICIAL INTELLIGENCE WITH VISUAL PROLOG

3.3.3.8.6.a - Create a Separate Window Object

You should now have 2 new items in your Project Tree under Package Lotto: 'HelpWindow.cl' and 'HelpWindow.pro'. Both will be quite limited for content and we will have to help them out. I'll provide abstracts for what you need to add to these files, as well as how you will need to modify the 'TaskWindow.pro' file.

◄ 124

## HelpWindow.cl

```
class helpWindow : window
  open core

predicates
  classInfo : core::classInfo.
  % @short Class information predicate.
  % @detail This predicate represents information predicate of this class
  % @end

constructors
  new : (window Parent, string Filename).

end class helpWindow
```

*Note: Objects need constructors to be created. Most languages provide destructors as well. All Objects in the Object Oriented Programming (OOP) world typically make use of 'new' to create objects during execution.*

## HelpWindow.pro

```
implement helpWindow
inherits documentwindow
  open core, lottoDomains, vpidomains, resourceidentifiers

constants
  className = "Lotto/helpWindow".
  classVersion = "".

  windowFlags : vpiDomains::wsflags = [wsf_SizeBorder, wsf_TitleBar,
    wsf_Maximize, wsf_Minimize, wsf_Close, wsf_ClipSiblings,
    wsf_ClipChildren].
  rectangle : vpiDomains::rct = rct(100, 80, 752, 462).
  menu : vpiDomains::menu = resMenu(id_TaskMenu).

clauses
  classInfo(className, classVersion).

facts
```

```
        filename : string.
        parent : window.
        isUnicode : boolean.

    clauses
        new(Parent, FileName) :-
            documentWindow::new(Parent),
            filename := FileName,
            parent := Parent,
            isUnicode := false.

    class predicates
        getFileContent : (
            string Filename,
            string InputStr,
            boolean IsUnicode) determ (i,o,o).

    clauses
        getFileContent("", "", true) :- !.
        getFileContent(FileName, InputStr, IsUnicode) :-
            InputStr = file::readString(FileName, IsUnicode).

        show():-
            getFileContent(filename, InputStr, IsUnicode), !,
            ReadOnly = b_false,
            Indent = b_true,
            InitPos = 1,
            isUnicode := IsUnicode,
            Font = vpi::fontCreate(ff_fixed, [], 8),
            HWND = vpiEditor::create(w_toplevel, rectangle, "", menu, parent:
            getvpiwindow(),
            windowFlags, Font, ReadOnly,
            Indent, InputStr, InitPos, geteventHandler()),
            vpi::winSetFont(HWND, Font).

        show():-
            vpiCommonDialogs::note(string::format("File <%s> does not exist",
            filename)).

    end implement helpWindow
```

## TaskWindow.pro (Abstract)

```
implement taskWindow
  inherits applicationWindow
  open core, vpiDomains, lottoDomains

clauses
  onHelpDownloadProcedure(Source, _MenuTag):-
  Form2 = help::new(This),
  Form2:show(),
  getNumbers::displayHelp(Help),
  Form2:set_form_text(Help),
  HelpWindow = helpWindow::new(Source, lottoHelpFile),
  HelpWindow:show().
```

When you rebuild the application with these changes, you will be asked if you want to add VpiEditor – click 'Add All". Then when you execute, you will see all 3 methods of providing the Help. However, you will not be able to get Help if the Numbers Form is on the screen. I'll show both examples below. Again, if you get any errors, check all of your typing - warnings are OK.

*Note: I've noticed there are times when it may be useful to go to the 'OBJ' directory maintained by Visual Prolog and delete all the entries (over 400 some entries), and that sometimes help clear up what may seem like mysterious compiler errors.*

The new Help window is still a child of the Task Window; however, you can scroll it individually even with the parent not maximized, and by default it puts black font text on a white background. If you only want one of these methods you will need to modify or comment out as necessary.

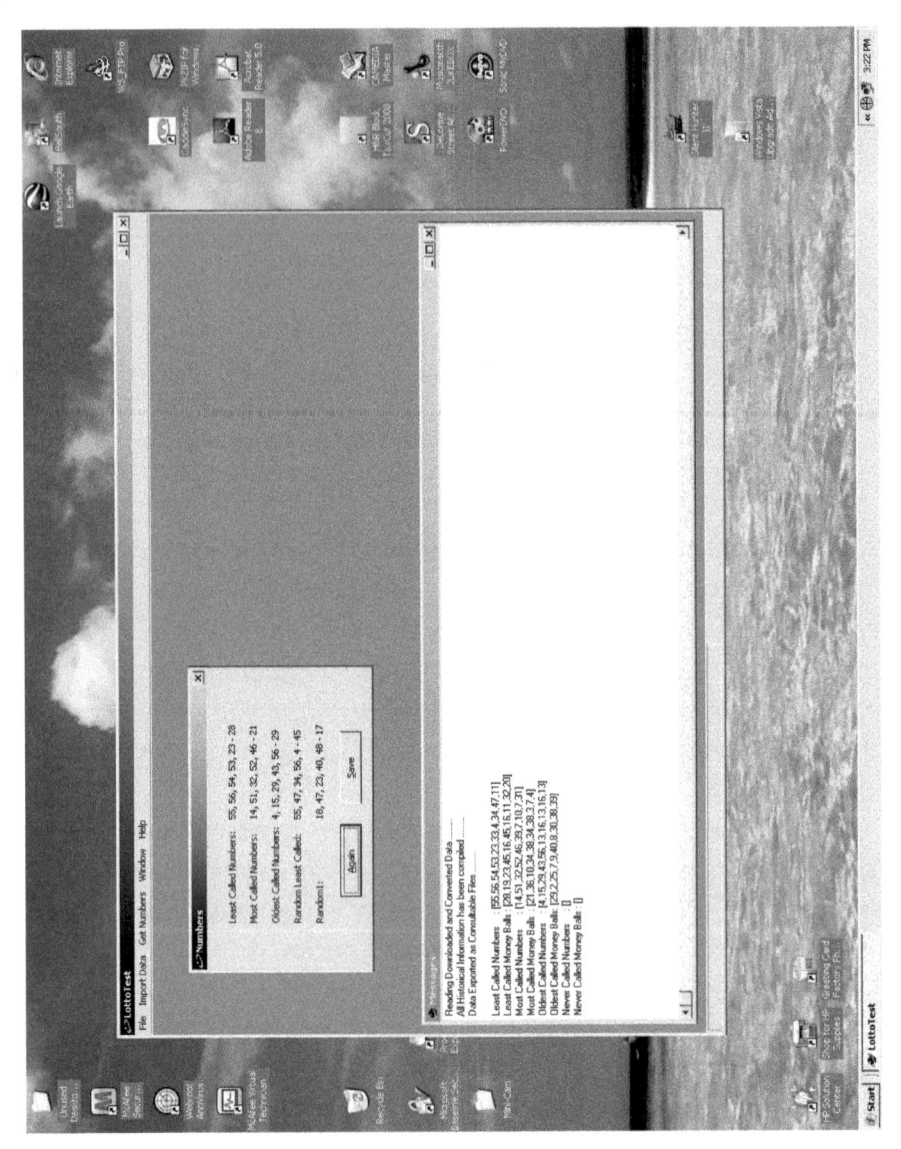

◄ A GUIDE TO ARTIFICIAL INTELLIGENCE WITH VISUAL PROLOG

3.3.3.8.6.b(1) - Application View [Import + Numbers]

◄ 128

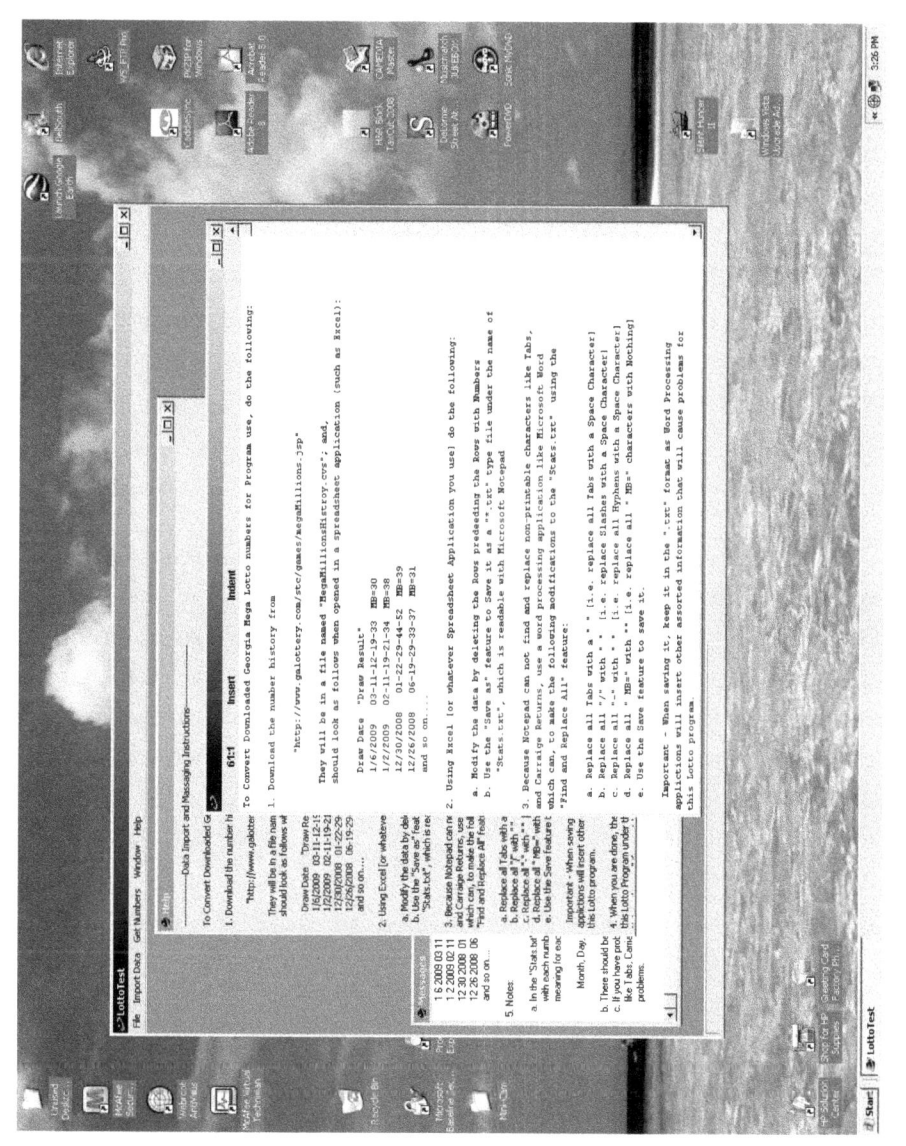

## SAMPLE APPLICATION ▶

**3.3.3.8.6.b(2) - Application View [Help]**

As a highlight though, you should notice that the methods used for the Message Window and the separate Window both do not require 'displayHelp()' to have an output parameter, only the Form for the Static Text Control. Also, the Message Window is the standard output for writing (unless you change it in your code) and the separate Window gets the information for the Window during initialization using the 'lottoHelpFile' constant from 'lottoDomains.cl'. Finally, you should have noticed the '_Source' parameter for 'openHelpDownloadProcedure()' was changed from an anonymous variable to a real variable, which in effect passes the parent handle to the child Window.

This should arm you sufficiently to engage your research in how to access the other assorted properties and methods for objects (that you create as well as those that Visual Prolog creates), without the assistance of a GUI Editor.

### 3.3.3.8.7 About Dialog

I could try to elaborate a little with abstracts from the 'AboutDialog.pro' with possible effects from using the Dialog GUI Editor, however, I'm not sure what properties you wanted to change other than maybe just the first line of Text. So I'll just show an example and recommend you explore it further maybe when and after you make changes. To open it in the Dialog GUI Editor double click on the 'AboutDialog.dlg' in the Project Tree. Click on which ever Static Text control you wish to change and change the Text in the Properties window.

SAMPLE APPLICATION

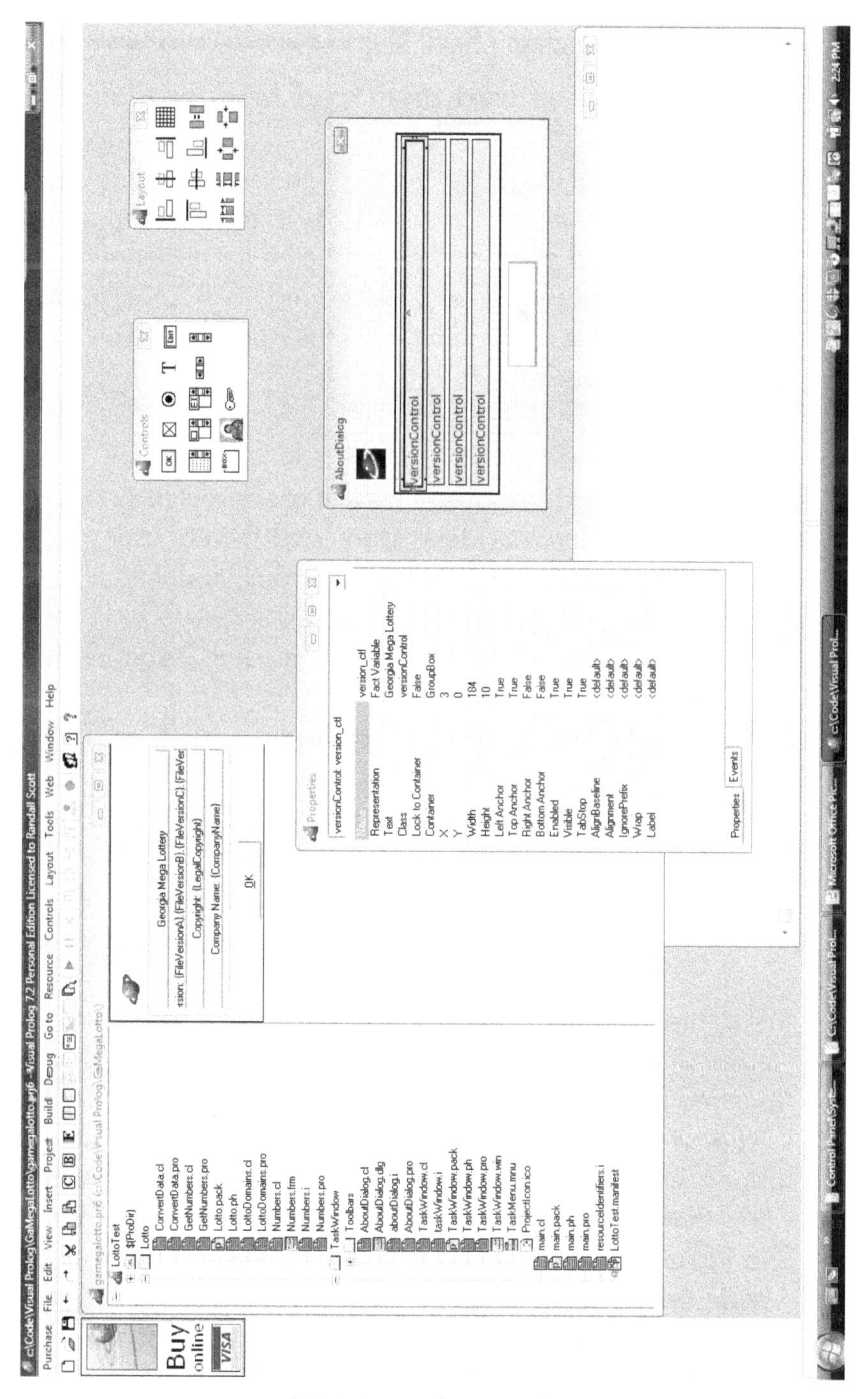

3.3.3.8.7 - About Dialog

## 3.4 Incremental Programming Road Map

The following can be used as a Road Map for Incremental Programming.

- *External Preparation*: Download the Mega Millions lottery information and prepare it as instructed for importation into the Application. Save it as 'Stats.txt' and don't forget to make a copy of it in the 'Exe' directory of the Application you create in Visual Prolog.

- *Application Development:*
    - CreateGAMegaLotto Project as instructed
    - Modify the TaskMenu Menu and Toolbar as instructed
    - Create the Lotto Package for your Modules:

        - LottoDomains – for all needed Global domains and constants
        - ConvertData – to do the import and history extraction
        - GetNumbers – mainly to deal with random numbers
        - Numbers – to display desired information
        - Help & HelpWindow – to provide User Help

- At a much lower level in each module, take one predicate at a time from the Predicate Section, and match it with all other needed predicates listed in its defining Clauses Section. Work with these predicate sets incrementally one-by-one, along with their referred to domains, facts and constants. Run them with Break Points set, so you can watch specific variables and facts change. Also make use of the Message Window to watch and track execution progress. Keep in mind, messages can be commented out or removed as your program progresses with good desired results.

- Visibility is forced by making predicates public when declared in the class declaration file '.cl'; and, private when they are declared in the class implementation file '.pro'. Visibility can also be somewhat affected by what you make part of the 'open' statement — at least from the aspect of using or not using the class scope identifier '::'.

## 3.5 Summary

In the process of building this application, I tried to give you exposure to a good methodology using concepts like Approach, Definition, and Design. We incrementally accomplished all of our goals; and, we covered all the key issues to application development using Visual Prolog.

My intent was to use a somewhat simple and interesting concept to build an application around, to help you learn some of the power of Artificial Intelligence (AI) using Visual Prolog; also, to give you some helpful insight to methodology when programming in a Declarative Computer Language. You should now have sufficient knowledge of the Visual Prolog Development suite and a comprehensive knowledge of the Visual Prolog modularity construction framework to build applications for just about anything. To give a more pictorial perspective of *module* or *object* predicate visibility, please refer to the following chart:

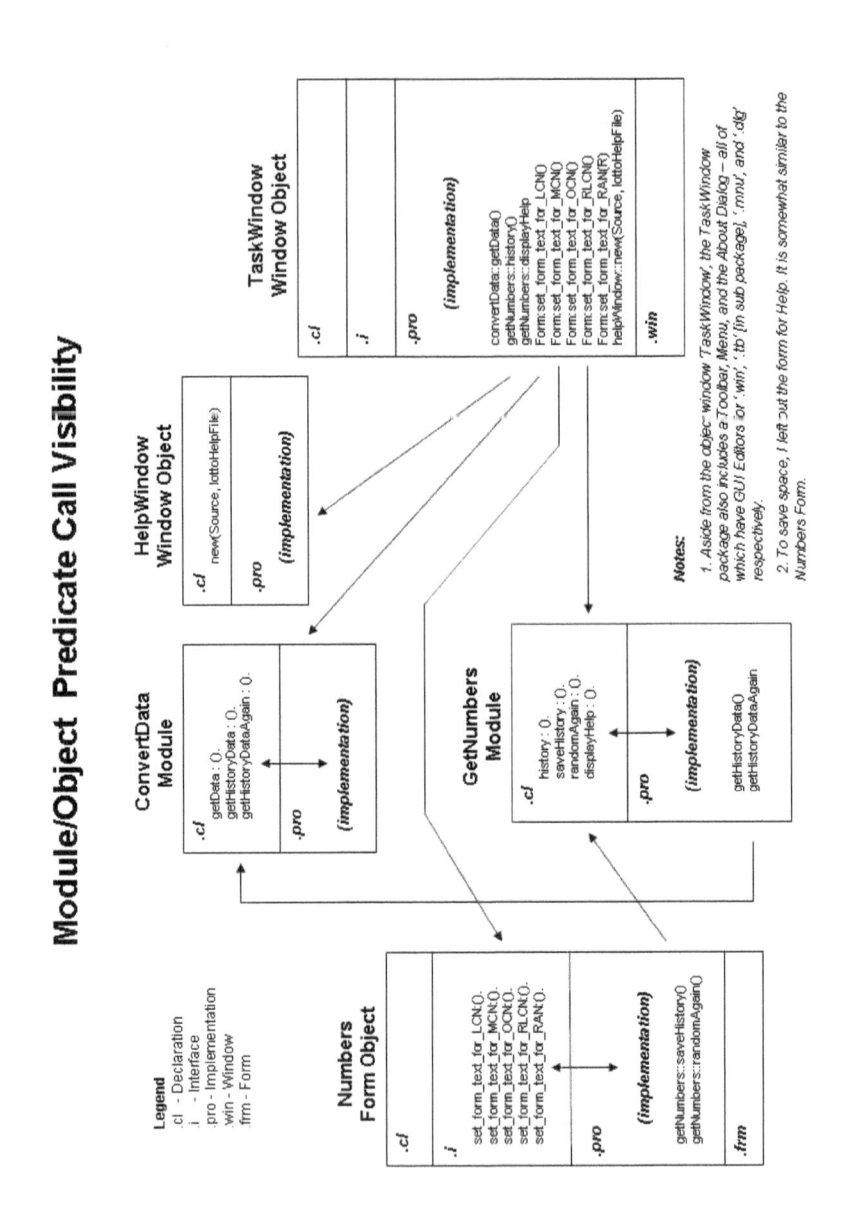

◀ A GUIDE TO ARTIFICIAL INTELLIGENCE WITH VISUAL PROLOG

## Module/Object Predicate Call Visibility

**Legend**
.cl - Declaration
.i - Interface
.pro - Implementation
.win - Window
.frm - Form

**ConvertData Module**
.cl: getData : O. getHistoryData : O. getHistoryDataAgain : O.
.pro: (implementation)

**HelpWindow Window Object**
.cl: new(Source, lottoHelpFile)
.pro: (implementation)

**TaskWindow Window Object**
.cl
.i
.pro: convertData::getData() getNumbers::history() getNumbers::displayHelp Form::set_form_text_for_LON() Form::set_form_text_for_MCN() Form::set_form_text_for_OCN() Form::set_form_text_for_RLCN() Form::set_form_text_for_RAN(R) helpWindow::new(Source, lottoHelpFile)
.win

**GetNumbers Module**
.cl: history : O. saveHistory : O. randomAgain : O. displayHelp : O.
.pro: (implementation) getHistoryData() getHistoryDataAgain()

**Numbers Form Object**
.cl
.i: set_form_text_for_LON(). set_form_text_for_MCN(). set_form_text_for_OCN(). set_form_text_for_RLCN(). set_form_text_for_RAN().
.pro: (implementation) getNumbers::saveHistory() getNumbers::randomAgain()
.frm

**Notes:**
1. Aside from the object window 'TaskWindow', the TaskWindow package also includes a Toolbar, Menu, and the About Dialog – all of which have GUI Editors for 'win', '.tb' (in sub package), '.mnu', and '.dlg' respectively.

2. To save space, I left out the form for Help. It is somewhat similar to the Numbers Form.

**3.4 - Predicate Call Visibility**

In the event you still have problems with the code that was incrementally added, I put the full file contents for the Modules, Forms, and Window that we created in the Reference Section. I did not list the entire contents of the 'AboutDialog.pro' files - mainly

◀ 134

the parts we affected through the GUI Editor or wrote source code ourselves. Keep in mind, all the source code listed, is presented as our somewhat finished product; which is missing the incremental steps we used as we went along. If you just copy the information from the reference section, you'll miss out on the incremental progression that was intended to help you develop skills. I recommend you follow the incremental process.

I would have preferred providing an accompanying CD with a copy of the Visual Prolog Personal Edition, and all the Source Code presented; however, my publisher does not currently support the CD included option. On the other hand, I will be communicating with the Visual Prolog PDC Staff to see if some of it can be made available on their Web Site for download.

In my introductory comments, I made a comment with reference to Visual Prolog following its predecessor Turbo Prolog "... with significant functionality added on; such as Object Oriented Programming, cross language integration, with fuzzy lines of integrating procedural functionality with declarative – I'll get into more detail on that later". You should have gathered knowledge about the Object Oriented Programming part by now; however, if your research and study hasn't flourished dicovery of the other 2 yet, I'll try to elaborate more.

Visual Prolog provides limited cross language integration; and, if you study the Language Reference Wiki under Foreign Language Code, you can get a lot more definitive information on how to do this. As far as the fuzzy lines of integrating procedural functionality with declarative, this seems to take place in more than one area; and, it depends on how you look at it. The ability to define *functions* as *predicates* is one. Another is the *procedure mode* and default for predicate declarations. And lastly, if you implement cross language integration, you are most likely going to integrate procedural functionality with declarative.

I only provided a relatively small and somewhat simple application to help teach quality application development methodology for the declarative language of Visual Prolog. Although I provided much source code for you with most of it explained, I deliberately avoided explaining all of it in hopes you would exercise your scholarly talent for independent inquisition and discovery. As you go through the process of writing source code in the Visual Prolog IDE, you should discover many of it great attributes, and particularly when you start dealing with their provided objects – streaming I/O is a good example when you assign it to a variable and start using a colon on it to access its methods or properties.

I think you should now be able to enjoy many of the great features offered by Visual Prolog, as you continue to expand your Artificial Intelligence horizons and application development skills. Personally, I think Visual Prolog is a gold mine of computer science AI genius, and fascinatingly full of excitement and discovery.

I know I have only touched on the near entry level part for potential participants in the Artificial Intellegence Community who may already enjoy Prolog, but mainly for those who want to join. At any rate, I certainly hope you enjoyed reading this book. I tried to make it somewhat entertaining as well; and, I hope other authors help build on the paper version of reference books for Visual Prolog. I like Visual Prolog, it has a global international audience, and I think it is growing in popularity.

CHAPTER **4**

# References

## 4.1 Built-in Predicates

The Built-in Operators, Constants, Domains, and Predicates which are listed in the Language Reference for version 7.2, are listed below only for convenience of having them on paper form as opposed to having to refer to them on your computer. These no doubt are subject to change as the product evolves. For more detail and clues to how they may be used, please refer to the Language Reference Book or on-line wiki.

**Operators**
Integral division

**Constants**

| | | |
|---|---|---|
| compilation_date | maxFloatDigits | platform_bits |
| compilation_time | null | platform_name |
| compiler_buildDate | nullHandle | |
| compiler_version | invalidHandle | |

## Domains

| | | |
|---|---|---|
| char | binaryNonAtomic | real32 |
| compareResult | integer | pointer |
| string | integer64 | handle |
| string8 | unsigned | boolean |
| symbol | unsigned64 | factDB |
| binary | real | |

## Predicates

| | | |
|---|---|---|
| assert | isErroneous | sourcefile_name |
| asserta | maxDigits | sourcefile_timestamp |
| assertz | not | succeed |
| bound | predicate_fullname | toBinary |
| class_Name | predicate_name | toBoolean |
| compare | retract | toString |
| convert | retractall | toTerm |
| digitsOf | retractFactDb | tryToTerm |
| errorExit | retractall | tryConvert |
| fail | sizeBitsOf | uncheckedConvert |
| free | sizeOf | upperBound |
| hasDomain | sizeOfDomain | |
| lowerBound | sourcefile_lineno | |

## 4.2 Program Foundation Class (PFC)

The Program Foundation Class of already constructed useful application oriented packages for Visual Prolog version 7.2, are listed below for convenience of having them in paper form, which also allows easy comparison of what comes with the Personal Edition Version and the Commercial Version. These no doubt are subject to change as the product evolves. For more detail and clues to how they may be used, please refer to the PFC references in the Visual Prolog Help. In addition, some examples are also provided and available for help.

# REFERENCES

| Commercial Version | Personal Edition Version |
|---|---|
| 5xVIP | |
| action | |
| application | application\Exe |
| binary | binary |
| boolean | boolean |
| cgi | |
| chainDB | |
| codePageId | |
| collection | |
| com | |
| console | |
| environment | |
| exception | exception |
| fileSystem | fileSystem |
| gui | gui |
| guid | |
| htmlHelp | |
| list | list |
| math | math |
| memory | memory |
| multithread | multiThread |
| namedValue | namedValue |
| odbc | |
| pie | |
| pipe | |
| ppStream | |
| prettyPrinter | |
| printing | |
| profile | |
| programControl | programControl |
| prologSyntax | |
| redBlackTree | |
| regExp | regExp |
| registry | registry |
| sendMail_smtp | |
| smapi | |
| std | std |
| stream | stream |
| string | string |
| string8 | string8 |
| systemTray | |

templateExpander   templateExpander
testSupport
time
vpi                vpi
windowsApi         windowsApi
disposable (interface)   disposable (interface)
runtimeLinkNamesRun (interface)   runtimeLinkNamesRun (interface)
core               core

## 4.3 Help Avenues

To get help learning Visual Prolog, the library is quite rich with resources. The only limiting factor is what you can find in written or Book form. Hopefully in time, that will be more abundant. Some people enjoy doing all their studying and research while on their computer; while others enjoy a mixture of Books as well as computers. I have no intention of repeating what is already available from the several resources you can find at the Visual Prolog Web Site. Aside from using this book, I recommend using the 'Beginners' Guide to Visual Prolog' as well as 'Visual Prolog for Tyros'. For each category and sub-category below, I will provide an example screen of what you should find when you reach that spot on your computer or the internet. Again, due to the fact that Visual Prolog is an evolving product, what you may find in time may differ some.

## 4.3.1 Built in Help

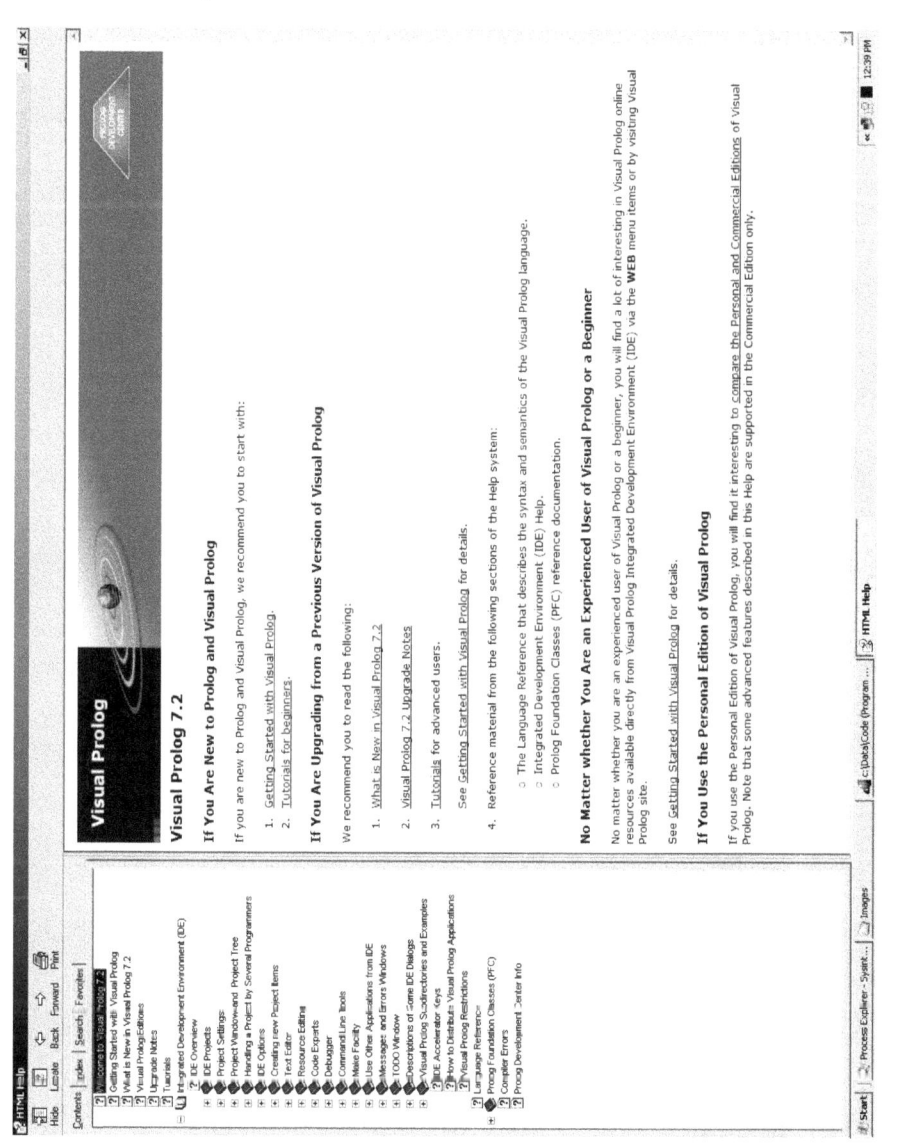

4.3.1 - Visual Prolog Help

### 4.3.2 PDC Resources on the Web

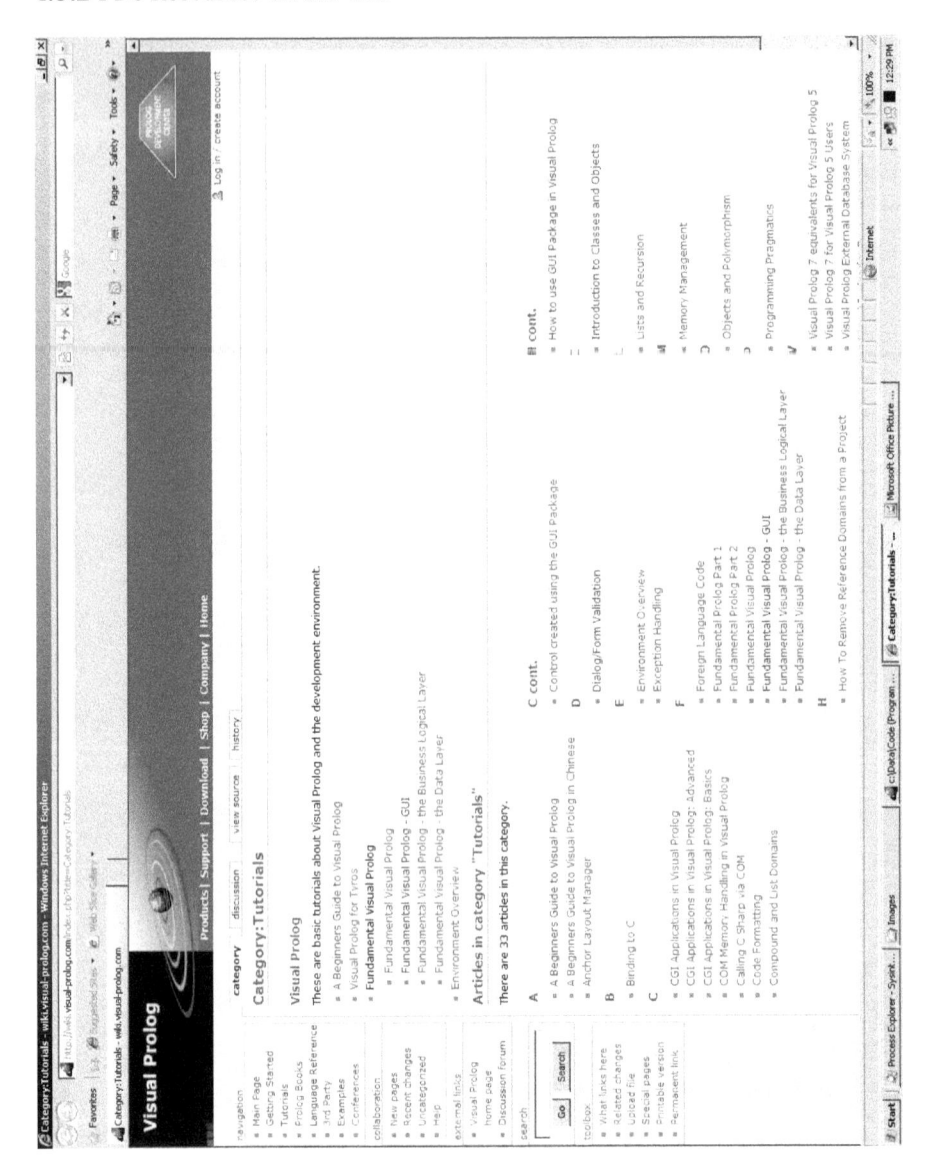

4.3.2 - Visual Prolog Tutorials

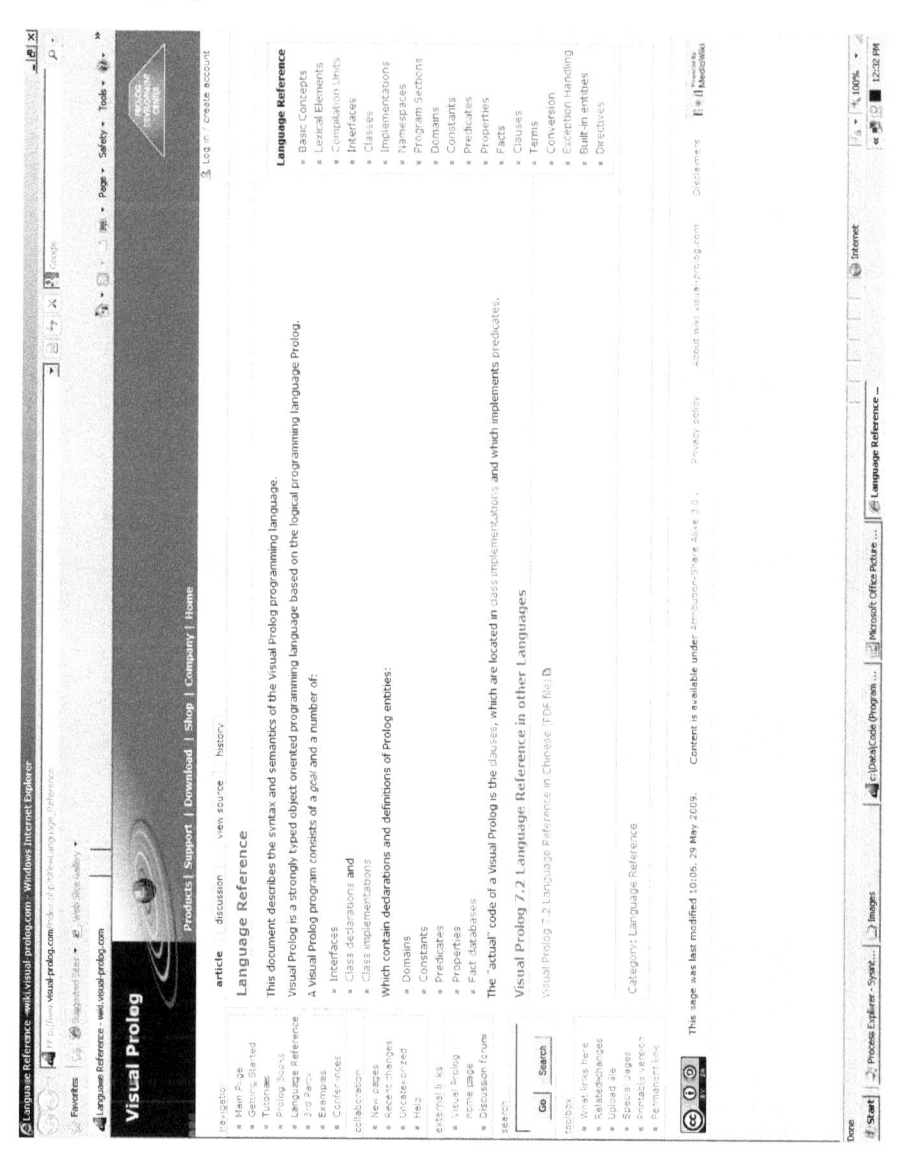

## REFERENCES

### 4.3.2.1 Language Reference Wiki

4.3.2.1 - Language Reference Wiki

## 4.3.2.2 Knowledge Base

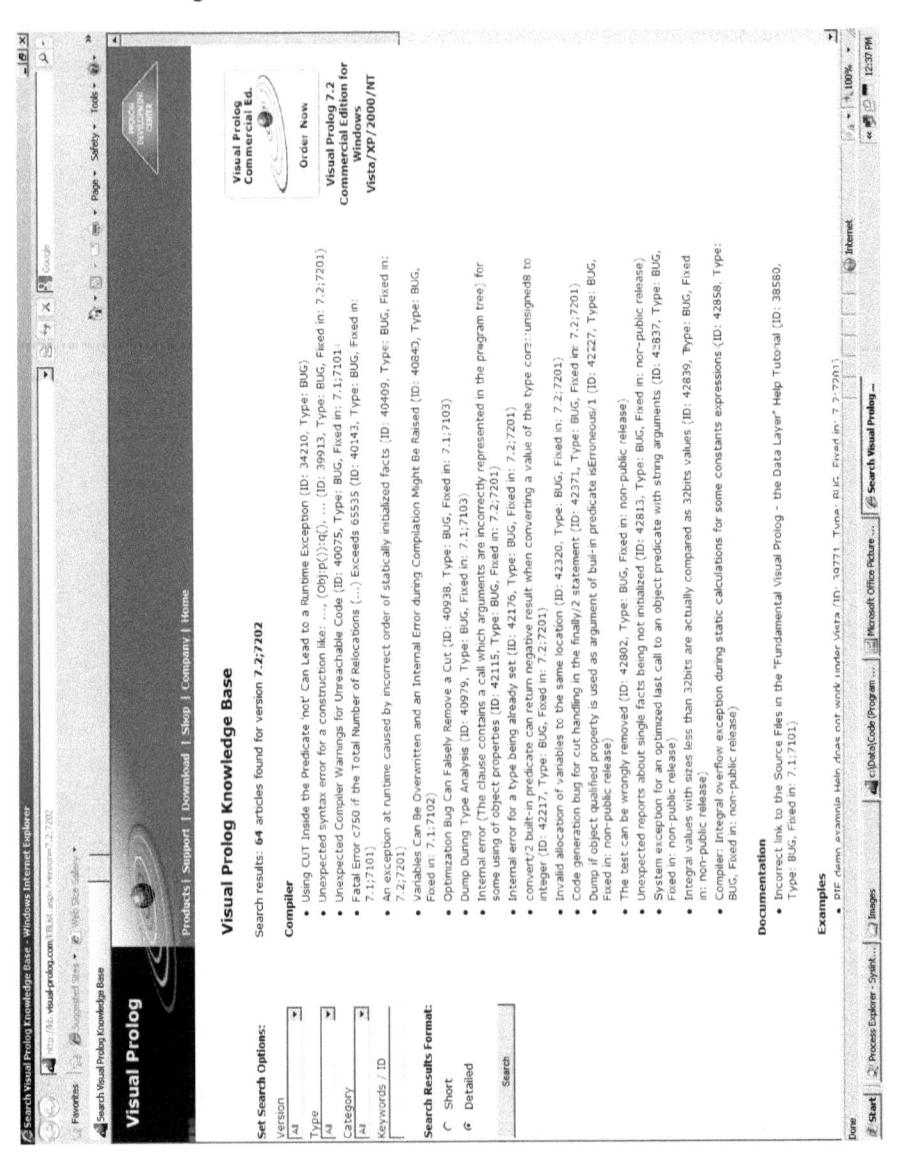

**4.3.2.2 - Knowledge Base**

## REFERENCES

### 4.3.2.3 Tutorials

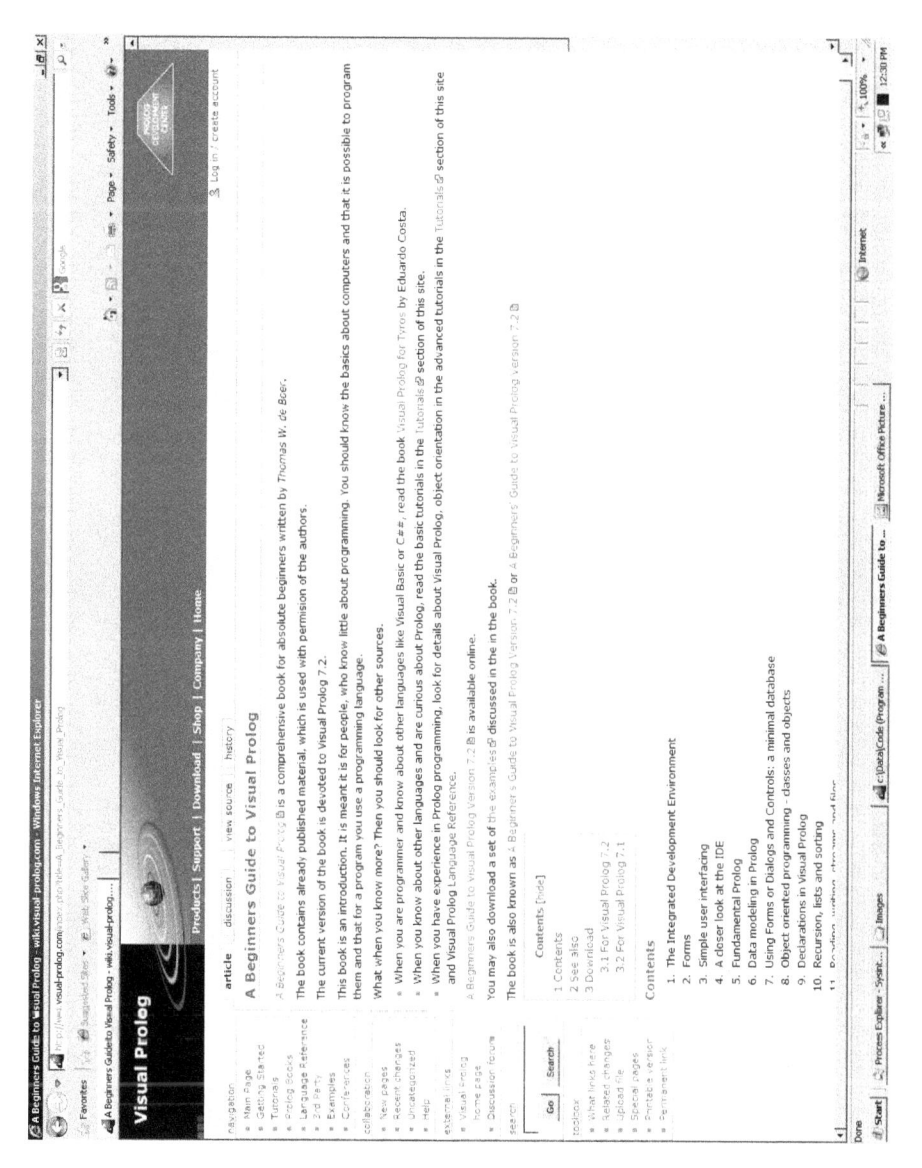

**4.3.2.3.a – Beginners' Guide to Visual Prolog (PDC Web)**

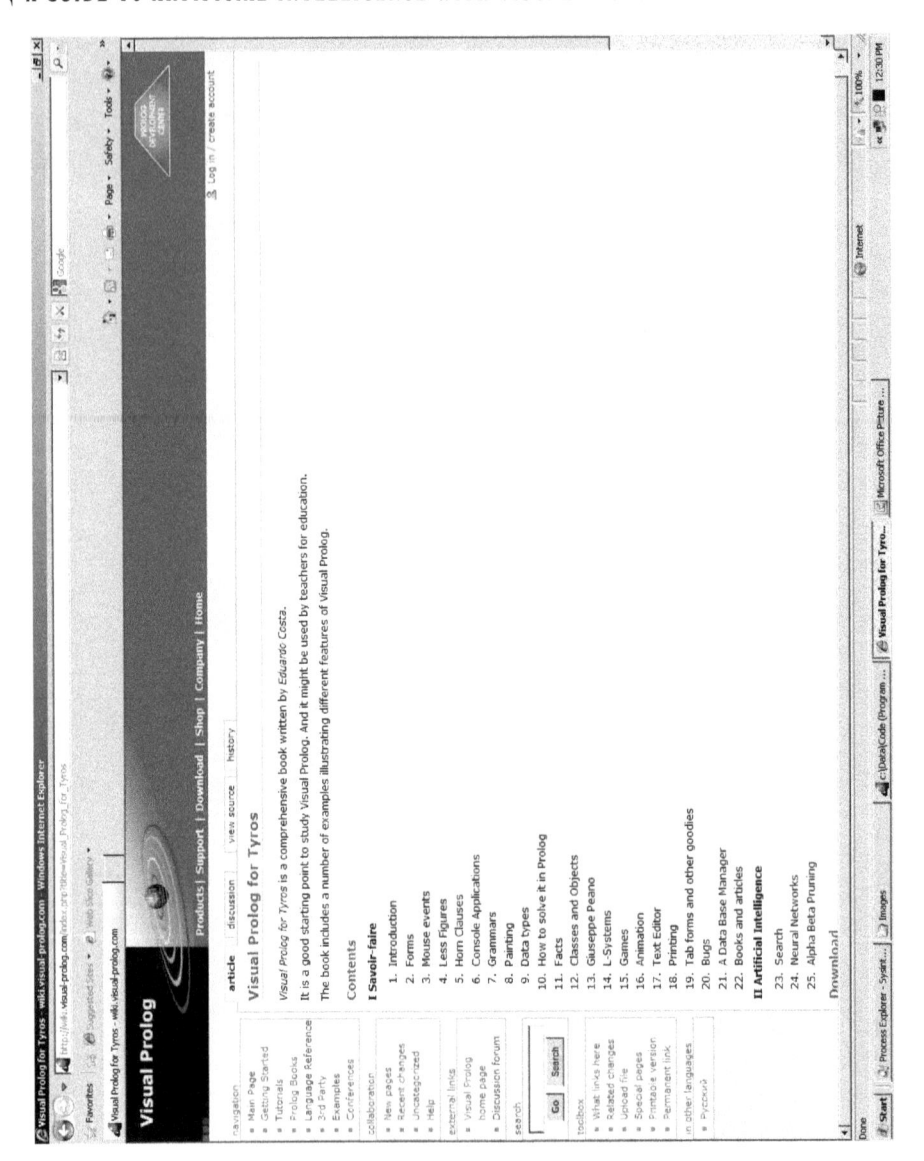

◀ A GUIDE TO ARTIFICIAL INTELLIGENCE WITH VISUAL PROLOG

4.3.2.3.b - Visual Prolog for Tyros (PDC Web)

◀ 146

# REFERENCES

### 4.3.2.4 Discussion Forum

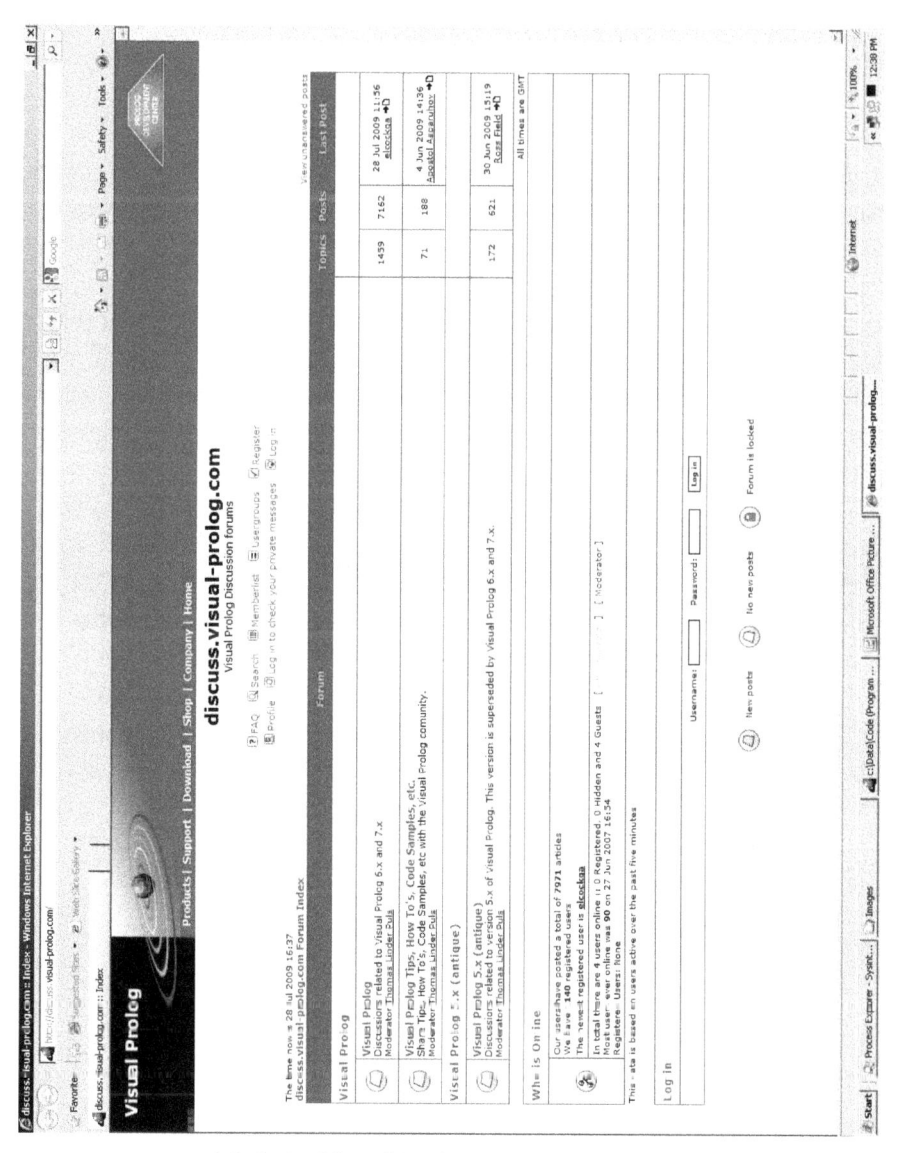

4.3.2.4 – Visual Prolog Discussion Forum

## 4.4 Source Code for Sample Application

It is important to know that if you plan to use all this Application

Source Code information instead of the incremental process described before, you will need to carefully blend the use of the GUI editors with the blocks of source code that affect them as well.

For example begin by making the necessary Menu and Toolbar corrections for TaskWindow (TaskWindow.mnu and ProjectToolbar.tb) including the effects of using the Code Expert with TaskWindow.win when you expand the menu and submenu items and double click them to force the GUI editor to place the sorce code place holders. Be sure to make all the GUI editing before modifying the .cl and .pro files. Also, when you get to the Numbers and Help Forms, again do all the needed activity with the Form GUI Editor before changing the source code in their .cl, .i, and .pro files. This includes all necessary Properties and Event settings in the GUI Editors. If you create the source code below before doing all the GUI Editor functions, you'll probably get some nasty compiler errors – mainly for what looks like duplicate place holders without source code. After a while, you will appreciate how the 2 (GUI Editor generated Source Code and maunually entered Source Code) interact with each other.

Also, it probably would be a good habit to periodically clean out all entries in the 'OBJ' directory before re-compiling or re-building.

### 4.4.1 LottoDomains.cl

```
class lottoDomains            % Name of the Class
    open core                 % Usually needed for everything you create

domains                       % Global Domains to be used
    year = integer.           % Lotto Data Imported: Year, Month, and Day
    month = integer.
    day = integer.
    number = integer.         % Generic use of Numbers
    fiveNumbers = integer*.   % List of 5 Numbers
    strList = string*.        % Generic List of String
    numData = num(number,
         number).             % Functor to Compound a number with info
    file = input; output.     % Used to deal with files
constants
```

## REFERENCES

```
lottoReadFile  = "Stats.txt".            % The hard coded name of
                                         % the download file
localData      = "LocalData.txt".        % Used to Localize Data for
                                         % the program
lottoDB        = "LottoData.txt".        % Imported Lotto Data in
                                         % format used by Prolog
lottoCntData   = "NumberCounts.txt".     % Information for program
                                         % verificaion analysis
lottoHistory   = "HistoryData.txt".      % Extracted Historical
                                         % Information.
lottoHelpFile  = "ImportInstructions.hlp". % File to be used to provide
                                         % User Help
lottoNumbers   = "LottoNumbers.txt".     % File use to Print History
                                         % and Random Numbers

% Number Balls   1-56    Numbers used for Regular Lotto Balls
% Money Ball     1-46    Numbers used for the Mega Money Ball

predicates
  classInfo : core::classInfo.
  % @short Class information  predicate.
  % @detail This predicate represents information predicate of this class.
  % @end

end class lottoDomains
```

### 4.4.2 LottoDomains.pro

```
implement lottoDomains
  open core

constants
  className = "Lotto/lottoDomains".
  classVersion = "".

clauses
  classInfo(className, classVersion).

end implement lottoDomains
```

# A GUIDE TO ARTIFICIAL INTELLIGENCE WITH VISUAL PROLOG

## 4.4.3 ConvertData.cl

```
class convertData
  open core, lottoDomains

predicates
  getData : ().        % We want this Predicate visible outside of convertData
  getHistoryData : (number*, number*, number*, number*, number*,
     number*, number*, number*)
       determ (o,o,o,o,o,o,o,o).
  getHistoryDataAgain : ().

  classInfo : core::classInfo.
  % @short Class information  predicate.
  % @detail This predicate represents information predicate of this class.
  % @end

end class convertData
```

## 4.4.4 ConvertData.pro

```
implement convertData
  open core, lottoDomains, string, list, file

class facts - localFacts      % Used for local static facts
  months: (integer, integer).

class facts - lottoData       % Converted 'Stats.txt' Lotto Data
  lotto : (year Year, month Month, day Day, number DateCP, fiveNumbers
FN, number MoneyBall).

class facts - lottoNumberData      % Temporary data elements used to
                                   % extract information
  numberCount : (numData X).       % Lotto Number and it's count
  numberDate : (numData X).        % Lotto Number and it's date
  moneyBallCount : (numData X).    % Money Ball Number and it's count
  moneyBallDate : (numData X).     % Money Ball Number and it's date
  nList : (number* X).             % A list of numbers
  ndList : (number* X).            % A list of dates
  mbList : (number* X).            % A list of Money Balls Numbers
  mbdList : (number* X).           % A list of Money Ball Number dates
  nnc : (number* X).               % A list of Numbers not counted
  mbnc : (number* X).              % A list of Money Ball Numbers not
                                   % counted
```

# REFERENCES

```
    lcn : (numData* LCN).            % A list of Least Called Numbers
    mcn: (numData* MCN).             % A list of Most Called Numbers
    lcmb : (numData* A).             % A list Of Least Called Money Balls
    mcmb : (numData* C).             % A list of Most Called Money Balls
    ocn : (numData* OCN).            % A list of Oldest Called Numbers
    ocmb : (numData* A).             % A list of Oldest Called Money Balls

  class facts - historyData          % Desired Historical Information
    numbersNeverCalled : (number* X).
    moneyBallsNeverCalled : (number* X).
    leastCalledNumbers : (number* LCN).
    mostCalledNumbers: (number* MCN).
    leastCalledMoneyBalls : (number* A).
    mostCalledMoneyBalls : (number* C).
    oldestCalledNumbers : (number* OCN).
    oldestCalledMoneyBalls : (number* A).

% Import Downloaded Data ---------------------
class predicates
    putData : () procedure.
    readData : (inputStream I) procedure (i).
    convStrList : (string Str, strList SL) procedure (i,o).
    getDate : (strList Str, year Y, month M, day D, number N) determ (i,o,o,o,o).
    getFiveNumbers : (strList SL, fiveNumbers N) determ (i,o).
    getMoneyBall : (strList SL, number N) determ (i,o).
    splitLine : (string Lotto, year Year, month Month, day Day, number DateCP,
        fiveNumbers FiveNumbers, number MoneyBall) determ (i,o,o,o,o,o,o).

% Inititial Data -------------------------------
class predicates
   initializeHistoryData : ().
   initNumbers : (number X, number Y).
   initMoneyBalls : (number X, number Y)
   getAllNumbers : ().
   fiveNumbers : (fiveNumbers X) determ (i).
   moneyBall : (number X) determ (i).
   dates : (number X, fiveNumbers Y, number Z) determ (i,i,i).
   setNumberDate: (number X, number Y) procedure (i,i).
   setMoneyBallDate : (number X, number Y) procedure (i,i).

% Get Significant Historical Data (i.e. Never Called, Most Called, Least
% Called, Oldest, etc. --------------
class predicates
   getHistory : ().
```

# A GUIDE TO ARTIFICIAL INTELLIGENCE WITH VISUAL PROLOG

```
    getLists : ().
    getNumbersNeverCalled : ().
    getMoneyBallsNeverCalled : ().
    getExtremeCalledNumbers : ().
    getExtremeCalledMoneyBalls : ().
    getOldestNumbers : ().
    getOldestMoneyBall : ().
    getTop10Numbers : (number* L, number* M).
    getTop10MoneyBalls : (number* L, number* M).
    getTop10OldestNumbers : (number* L).
    getTop10OldestMoneyBalls : (number* L).

clauses
% To retrieve History Data from outside of the ConvertData Class
    getHistoryData(LCN, LCMB, MCN, MCMB, OCN, OCMB, NCN, NCMB) :-
        numbersNeverCalled(NCN),
        moneyBallsNeverCalled(NCMB),
        leastCalledNumbers(LCN),
        mostCalledNumbers(MCN),
        leastCalledMoneyBalls(LCMB),
        mostCalledMoneyBalls(MCMB),
        oldestCalledNumbers(OCN),
        oldestCalledMoneyBalls(OCMB), !.

    getHistoryDataAgain() :-
        consult("HistoryData.txt", historyData), !.

% Import Downloaded Data --------------------------------

    getData() :-
        stdio::write("Reading Downloaded and Converted Data ........\n"),
        I = inputStream_file::openFile8(lottoReadFile),
        readData(I),
        %stdio::write("Download Data Acquired ........ \n"),
        initializeHistoryData,
        % stdio::write("All Numbers, Money Balls, and their Dates have been
        % Initialized ........\n"),
        getAllNumbers,
        % stdio::write("All Numbers and Money Balls have been Counted
        % ........\n"),
        % stdio::write("All Dates Called have been Normalized ........\n"),
        getHistory,
        stdio::write("All Historical Information has been compiled ........\n"),
        putData,
```

## REFERENCES

```
      stdio::write("Data Exported as Consultable Files ........\n\n"), !.

  readData(I) :-
    not(I:endOfStream()),
    Lotto = I:readLine(),
    splitLine(Lotto, Year, Month, Day, DateCP, FiveNumbers, MoneyBall),
    assertz(lotto(Year, Month, Day, DateCP, FiveNumbers, MoneyBall)),
    readData(I),
    fail.
  readData(_):-!.

  putData() :-
    % file::save(localData, localFacts),
    % file::save(lottoCntData, lottoNumberData),
    file::save(lottoDB, lottoData),
    file::save(lottoHistory, historyData), !.

  splitLine(Lotto, Year, Month, Day, DateCP, FiveNumbers, MoneyBall) :-
    convStrList(Lotto,SL),
    getDate(SL, Year, Month, Day, DateCP),
    getFiveNumbers(SL, FiveNumbers),
    getMoneyBall(SL, MoneyBall), !.

  convStrList(Str, [H|T]) :-
    frontToken(Str,H,Str1), ! ,
    convStrList(Str1,T).
  convStrList(_,[]).

% --------- M,D,Y,1,2,3,4,5,M -----------
  getDate([X,Y,Z,_,_,_,_,_,_], Year, Month, Day, DateCP) :-
    Month = toTerm(month, X),
    months(Month, Count),
    Day = toTerm(day, Y),
    Year = toTerm(year, Z),
    DateCP = ((Year-2000)*1000) + Count + Day,!.

  getFiveNumbers([_,_,_,A,B,C,D,E,_],FiveNumbers) :-
    Z = toTerm(number, A),
    Y = toTerm(number, B),
    X = toTerm(number, C),
    W = toTerm(number, D),
    V = toTerm(number, E),
    FiveNumbers = [Z,Y,X,W,V], !.
```

### A GUIDE TO ARTIFICIAL INTELLIGENCE WITH VISUAL PROLOG

```
        getMoneyBall([_,_,_,_,_,_,_,X], MoneyBall) :-
          M = toTerm(number, X),
          MoneyBall = M.

    months(1, 0).
    months(2, 31).
    months(3, 60).
    months(4, 91).
    months(5, 121).
    months(6, 152).
    months(7, 182).
    months(8, 213).
    months(9, 244).
    months(10, 274).
    months(11, 305).
    months(12, 335).

% Inititial Data --------------------------------------
clauses
  initializeHistoryData() :-
      initNumbers(1,0),
      initMoneyBalls(1,0),!.

  initNumbers(57, _) :- !.
    % stdio::write("Number Counts have been Initialized ........\n"), !.
  initNumbers(X, Y) :-
    assertz(numberCount(num(X,Y))),
    assertz(numberDate(num(X,Y))),
    NewX = X + 1,
    initNumbers(NewX, Y).

  initMoneyBalls(47, _) :- !.
    % stdio::write("Money Ball Counts have been Initialized ........\n"), !.
  initMoneyBalls(X, Y) :-
    assertz(moneyBallCount(num(X,Y))),
    assertz(moneyBallDate(num(X,Y))),
    NewX = X + 1,
    initMoneyBalls(NewX, Y).


    getAllNumbers() :-
      lotto(_,_,_,W,X,Y),
      fiveNumbers(X),
      moneyBall(Y),
```

```
    dates(W,X,Y),
    fail.
 getAllNumbers() :- !.

fiveNumbers([A,B,C,D,E]) :-
   retract(numberCount(num(A,OldC1))),
   NewC1 = OldC1 + 1,
   assertz(numberCount(num(A,NewC1))),
   %-----------------------------------------
   retract(numberCount(num(B,OldC2))),
   NewC2 = OldC2 + 1,
   assertz(numberCount(num(B,NewC2))),
   %-----------------------------------------
   retract(numberCount(num(C,OldC3))),
   NewC3 = OldC3 + 1,
   assertz(numberCount(num(C,NewC3))),
   %-----------------------------------------
   retract(numberCount(num(D,OldC4))),
   NewC4 = OldC4 + 1,
   assertz(numberCount(num(D,NewC4))),
   %-----------------------------------------
   retract(numberCount(num(E,OldC5))),
   NewC5 = OldC5 + 1,
   assertz(numberCount(num(E,NewC5))),!.

moneyBall(A):-
   retract(moneyBallCount(num(A,X))),
   Y = X+1,
   assertz(moneyBallCount(num(A,Y))),!.

dates(Date,[A,B,C,D,E],MB):-
   setNumberDate(Date, A),
   setNumberDate(Date, B),
   setNumberDate(Date, C),
   setNumberDate(Date, D),
   setNumberDate(Date, E),
   setMoneyBallDate(Date,MB).

setNumberDate(Date1, X) :-
   numberDate(num(X, Date0)),
   Date1 > Date0,
   retract(numberDate(num(X, Date0))),
   assertz(numberDate(num(X, Date1))),!.
setNumberDate(_, _) :- !.
```

## ◄ A GUIDE TO ARTIFICIAL INTELLIGENCE WITH VISUAL PROLOG

```
setMoneyBallDate(Date1, X) :-
  moneyBallDate(num(X, DateO)),
  Date1 > DateO,
  retract(moneyBallDate(num(X, DateO))),
  assertz(moneyBallDate(num(X, Date1))),!.
setMoneyBallDate(_, _) :- !.

% Get Significant Historical Data (i.e. Most Called, Least Called, Oldest,
% etc. --------------
clauses
  getHistory() :-
      getLists,
      getNumbersNeverCalled,
      getMoneyBallsNeverCalled,
      getExtremeCalledNumbers,
      getExtremeCalledMoneyBalls,
      getOldestNumbers,
      getOldestMoneyBall, !.

  getLists():-
      findall(W, numberCount(num(_,W)), List1),
      findall(X, numberDate(num(_,X)), List2),
      findall(Y, moneyBallCount(num(_,Y)), List3),
      findall(Z, moneyBallDate(num(_,Z)), List4),
      assertz(nList(List1)),
      assertz(ndList(List2)),
      assertz(mbList(List3)),
      assertz(mbdList(List4)), !.

  getNumbersNeverCalled() :-
      findall(N, (numberCount(num(N, C)), C=0), List),
      assert(nnc(List)),
      assert(numbersNeverCalled(List)).

  getMoneyBallsNeverCalled():-
      findall(N, (moneyBallCount(num(N, C)), C=0), List),
      assert(mbnc(List)),
      assert(moneyBallsNeverCalled(List)).

  getExtremeCalledNumbers():-
      retract(nList(C)),
      L = list::sort(C, ascending),
      M = list::sort(C, descending),
      getTop10Numbers(L, M),!.
```

## REFERENCES

```
getExtremeCalledNumbers():-!.

getExtremeCalledMoneyBalls() :-
    retract(mbList(C)),
    L = list::sort(C, ascending),
    M = list::sort(C, descending),
    getTop10MoneyBalls(L, M),!.
getExtremeCalledMoneyBalls().

getOldestNumbers() :-
    retract(ndList(C)),
    L = list::sort(C, descending),
    getTop10OldestNumbers(L),!.
getOldestNumbers().

getOldestMoneyBall() :-
    retract(mbdList(C)),
    L = list::sort(C, descending),
    getTop10OldestMoneyBalls(L),!.
getOldestMoneyBall().

getTop10Numbers([L1, L2, L3, L4, L5, L6, L7, L8, L9, L10 | _],
                [M1, M2, M3, M4, M5, M6, M7, M8, M9, M10|_] ) :-
    numberCount(num(A1, L1)),
    numberCount(num(A2, L2)),
    A1 <> A2,
    numberCount(num(A3, L3)),
    A3 <> A2, A3 <> A1,
    numberCount(num(A4, L4)),
    A4 <> A3, A4 <> A2, A4 <> A1,
    numberCount(num(A5, L5)),
    A5 <> A4, A5 <> A3, A5<> A2, A5 <> A1,
    numberCount(num(A6, L6)),
    A6 <> A5,
    numberCount(num(A7, L7)),
    A7 <> A6,
    numberCount(num(A8, L8)),
    A8 <> A7,
    numberCount(num(A9, L9)),
    A9 <> A8,
    numberCount(num(A10, L10)),
    A10 <> A9,
```

◄ A GUIDE TO ARTIFICIAL INTELLIGENCE WITH VISUAL PROLOG

```
        LCNL  = [num(A1, L1), num(A2, L2), num(A3, L3), num(A4, L4),
                num(A5, L5),
                num(A6, L6), num(A7, L7), num(A8, L8), num(A9, L9),
                num(A10, L10)],
        LCNS  = [A1, A2, A3, A4, A5, A6, A7, A8, A9, A10],
        assertz(lcn(LCNL)),
        assertz(leastCalledNumbers(LCNS)),

        numberCount(num(B1, M1)),
        numberCount(num(B2, M2)),
        B1 <> B2,
        numberCount(num(B3, M3)),
        B3 <> B2, B3 <> B1,
        numberCount(num(B4, M4)),
        B4 <> B3, B4 <> B2, B4 <> B1,
        numberCount(num(B5, M5)),
        B5 <> B4, B5 <> B3, B5 <> B2, B5 <> B1,
        numberCount(num(B6, M6)),
        B6 <> B5,
        numberCount(num(B7, M7)),
        B7 <> B6,
        numberCount(num(B8, M8)),
        B8 <> B7,
        numberCount(num(B9, M9)),
        B9 <> B8,
        numberCount(num(B10, M10)),
        B10 <> B9,
        MCNL  = [num(B1, M1), num(B2, M2), num(B3, M3), num(B4,
                M4), num(B5, M5),
                num(B6, M6), num(B7, M7), num(B8, M8), num(B9, M9),
                num(B10, M10)],
        MCNS  = [B1, B2, B3, B4, B5, B6, B7, B8, B9, B10],
        assertz(mcn(MCNL)),
        assertz(mostCalledNumbers(MCNS)), !.
getTop10Numbers(_,_).

        getTop10MoneyBalls([L1, L2, L3, L4, L5, L6, L7, L8, L9, L10 | _],
                [M1, M2, M3, M4, M5, M6, M7, M8, M9,
                M10|_] ) :-
        moneyBallCount(num(A1, L1)),
        moneyBallCount(num(A2, L2)),
        A1 <> A2,
        moneyBallCount(num(A3, L3)),
        A3 <> A2, A3 <> A1,
```

◄ 158

## REFERENCES

```
moneyBallCount(num(A4, L4)),
A4 <> A3, A4 <> A2, A4 <> A1,
moneyBallCount(num(A5, L5)),
A5 <> A4, A5 <> A3, A5 <> A2, A5 <> A1,
moneyBallCount(num(A6, L6)),
A6 <> A5,
moneyBallCount(num(A7, L7)),
A7 <> A6,
moneyBallCount(num(A8, L8)),
A8 <> A7,
moneyBallCount(num(A9, L9)),
A9 <> A8,
moneyBallCount(num(A10, L10)),
A10 <> A9,
LCMBL  = [num(A1, L1), num(A2, L2), num(A3, L3), num(A4, L4),
          num(A5, L5),
          num(A6, L6), num(A7, L7), num(A8, L8), num(A9, L9),
          num(A10, L10)],
LCMBS  = [A1, A2, A3, A4, A5, A6, A7, A8, A9, A10],
assertz(lcmb(LCMBL)),
assertz(leastCalledMoneyBalls(LCMBS)),

moneyBallCount(num(B1, M1)),
moneyBallCount(num(B2, M2)),
B1 <> B2,
moneyBallCount(num(B3, M3)),
B3 <> B2, B3 <> B1,
moneyBallCount(num(B4, M4)),
B4 <> B3, B4 <> B2, B4 <> B1,
moneyBallCount(num(B5, M5)),
B5 <> B4, B5 <> B3, B5 <> B2, B5 <> B1,
moneyBallCount(num(B6, M6)),
B6 <> B5,
moneyBallCount(num(B7, M7)),
B7 <> B6,
moneyBallCount(num(B8, M8)),
B8 <> B7,
moneyBallCount(num(B9, M9)),
B9 <> B8,
moneyBallCount(num(B10, M10)),
B10 <> B9,
MCMBL  = [num(B1, M1), num(B2, M2), num(B3, M3), num(B4,
            M4), num(B5, M5),
```

### A GUIDE TO ARTIFICIAL INTELLIGENCE WITH VISUAL PROLOG

```
                num(B6, M6), num(B7, M7), num(B8, M8), num(B9,
                M9), num(B10, M10)],
    MCMBS   = [B1, B2, B3, B4, B5, B6, B7, B8, B9, B10],
    assertz(mcmb(MCMBL)),
    assertz(mostCalledMoneyBalls(MCMBS)), !.
getTop10MoneyBalls(_,_).

getTop10OldestNumbers([L1, L2, L3, L4, L5, L6, L7, L8, L9, L10 | _]):-
    numberDate(num(A1, L1)),
    numberDate(num(A2, L2)),
    A1 <> A2,
    numberDate(num(A3, L3)),
    A3 <> A2, A3 <> A1,
    numberDate(num(A4, L4)),
    A4 <> A3, A4 <> A2, A4 <> A1,
    numberDate(num(A5, L5)),
    A5 <> A4, A5 <> A3, A5 <> A2, A5 <> A1,
    numberDate(num(A6, L6)),
    A6 <> A5,
    numberDate(num(A7, L7)),
    A7 <> A6,
    numberDate(num(A8, L8)),
    A8 <> A7,
    numberDate(num(A9, L9)),
    A9 <> A8,
    numberDate(num(A10, L10)),
    A10 <> A9,
    OCNL  = [num(A1, L1), num(A2, L2), num(A3, L3), num(A4, L4),
            num(A5, L5),
            num(A6, L6), num(A7, L7), num(A8, L8), num(A9, L9),
            num(A10, L10)],
    OCNS  = [A1, A2, A3, A4, A5, A6, A7, A8, A9, A10],
    assertz(ocn(OCNL)),
    assertz(oldestCalledNumbers(OCNS)),!.
getTop10OldestNumbers(_).

getTop10OldestMoneyBalls([L1, L2, L3, L4, L5, L6, L7, L8, L9, L10 | _]):-
    moneyBallDate(num(A1, L1)),
    moneyBallDate(num(A2, L2)),
    A1 <> A2,
    moneyBallDate(num(A3, L3)),
    A3 <> A2, A3 <> A1,
    moneyBallDate(num(A4, L4)),
    A4 <> A3, A4 <> A2, A4 <> A1,
```

## REFERENCES

```
        moneyBallDate(num(A5, L5)),
        A5 <> A4, A5 <> A3, A5 <> A2, A5 <> A1,
        moneyBallDate(num(A6, L6)),
        A6 <> A5,
        moneyBallDate(num(A7, L7)),
        A7 <> A6,
        moneyBallDate(num(A8, L8)),
        A8 <> A7,
        moneyBallDate(num(A9, L9)),
        A9 <> A8,
        moneyBallDate(num(A10, L10)),
        A10 <> A9,
        OCMBL  = [num(A1, L1), num(A2, L2), num(A3, L3), num(A4, L4),
                  num(A5, L5),
                  num(A6, L6), num(A7, L7), num(A8, L8), num(A9, L9),
                  num(A10, L10)],
        OCMBS  = [A1, A2, A3, A4, A5, A6, A7, A8, A9, A10],
        assertz(ocmb(OCMBL)),
        assertz(oldestCalledMoneyBalls(OCMBS)), !.
getTop10OldestMoneyBalls(_).

constants
    className = "Lotto/convertData".
    classVersion = "".

clauses
    classInfo(className, classVersion).

end implement convertData
```

## 4.4.5 GetNumbers.cl

```
class getNumbers
    open core, lottoDomains, convertData

predicates
    history : (string*) procedure ([o, o, o, o, o]).
    saveHistory : ().
    randomAgain : (string, string) procedure (o, o).
    displayHelp : (string) procedure (o).

    classInfo : core::classInfo.
    % @short Class information  predicate.
```

### A GUIDE TO ARTIFICIAL INTELLIGENCE WITH VISUAL PROLOG

% @detail This predicate represents information predicate of this class.
% @end

end class getNumbers

## 4.4.6 GetNumbers.pro

```
implement getNumbers
   open core, lottoDomains, convertData, file, string, math, list

constants
   className = "Lotto/getNumbers".
   classVersion = "".

class facts - displayNumbers
   leastCalledNumbers : (string LCN).
   mostCalledNumbers: (string MCN).
   oldestCalledNumbers : (string OCN).
   leastCalledRandom : (string LCR).
   randomLotto1 : (string RL1).

class facts - tempLocal
   regularNumbers    : (number* RN).
   moneyBallNumbers : (number* MBN).

class predicates

   historyDataConvert : (number*, number*, number*, number*, number*,
   number*) determ (i, i, i, i, i, i).
   convertListToString : (number*, number*, string) determ (i, i, o).
   get_Random_LCN : (number*, number*).
   get_Random : ().
%   getHelp : (inputStream I) multi (i).

clauses

   history (DisplayData):-
      existFile("LottoData.txt"),
      getHistoryData(LCN, LCMB, MCN, MCMB, OCN, OCMB, NCN, NCMB),
      historyDataConvert(LCN, LCMB, MCN, MCMB, OCN, OCMB),
      get_Random_LCN(LCN, LCMB),
      get_Random(),
      leastCalledNumbers(S1),
```

## REFERENCES

```
    mostCalledNumbers(S2),
    oldestCalledNumbers(S3),
    leastCalledRandom(S4),
    randomLotto1(S5),
    DisplayData = [S1, S2, S3, S4, S5],
    stdio::write("Least Called Numbers     : ", LCN, "\n"),
    stdio::write("Least Called Money Balls : ", LCMB, "\n"),
    stdio::write("Most Called Numbers      : ", MCN, "\n"),
    stdio::write("Most Called Money Balls  : ", MCMB, "\n"),
    stdio::write("Oldest Called Numbers    : ", OCN, "\n"),
    stdio::write("Oldest Called Money Balls: ", OCMB, "\n"),
    stdio::write("Never Called Numbers     : ", NCN, "\n"),
    stdio::write("Never Called Money Balls : ", NCMB, "\n\n\n"), !.

history (DisplayData):-
    existFile("LottoData.txt"),
    getHistoryDataAgain,
    getHistoryData(LCN, LCMB, MCN, MCMB, OCN, OCMB, NCN, NCMB),
    historyDataConvert(LCN, LCMB, MCN, MCMB, OCN, OCMB),
    get_Random_LCN(LCN, LCMB),
    get_Random(),
    leastCalledNumbers(S1),
    mostCalledNumbers(S2),
    oldestCalledNumbers(S3),
    leastCalledRandom(S4),
    randomLotto1(S5),
    DisplayData = [S1, S2, S3, S4, S5],
    stdio::write("Least Called Numbers     : ", LCN, "\n"),
    stdio::write("Least Called Money Balls : ", LCMB, "\n"),
    stdio::write("Most Called Numbers      : ", MCN, "\n"),
    stdio::write("Most Called Money Balls  : ", MCMB, "\n"),
    stdio::write("Oldest Called Numbers    : ", OCN, "\n"),
    stdio::write("Oldest Called Money Balls: ", OCMB, "\n"),
    stdio::write("Never Called Numbers     : ", NCN, "\n"),
    stdio::write("Never Called Money Balls : ", NCMB, "\n\n\n"), !.

history (["", "", "", "", ""]):-
    stdio::write("Data Has Not been imported - Import data First \n\n" ),!.

get_Random_LCN(LCN, LCMB):-
    N1 = tryGetNth(math::random(9), LCN),
    N2 = tryGetNth(math::random(9), LCN),
    N2 <> N1,
    N3 = tryGetNth(math::random(9), LCN),
```

## A GUIDE TO ARTIFICIAL INTELLIGENCE WITH VISUAL PROLOG

```
       N3 <> N2, N3 <> N1,
       N4 = tryGetNth(math::random(9), LCN),
       N4 <> N3, N4 <> N2, N4 <> N1,
       N5 = tryGetNth(math::random(9), LCN),
       N5 <> N4, N5 <> N3, N5 <> N2, N5 <> N1,
       RandLCN = [N1, N2, N3, N4, N5],
       RandLCMB = tryGetNth(math::random(9), LCMB),
       convertListToString(RandLCN, [RandLCMB], S),
       assert(leastCalledRandom(S)), !.
    get_Random_LCN(LCN, LCMB):- get_Random_LCN(LCN, LCMB).

    get_Random():-
       assert(regularNumbers([ 1, 2, 3, 4, 5, 6, 7, 8, 9,10,11,12,13,14,
                        15,16,17,18,19,20,21,22,23,24,25,26,27,
                        28,29,30, 31,32,33,34,35,36,37,38,39,
                        40,41,42,43,44,45,46,47,48,49,50,51,52,
                        53,54,55,56])),
       assert(moneyBallNumbers([ 1, 2, 3, 4, 5, 6, 7, 8, 9,10,11,12,13,14,
                        15,16,17,18,19,20,21,22,23,24, 25,26,
                        27,28,29,30,31,32,33,34,35,36,37,38,
                        39,40,41,42,43,44,45,46])),
       regularNumbers(Ns),
       moneyBallNumbers(MBs),
       N1 = tryGetNth(math::random(55)+1, Ns),
       N2 = tryGetNth(math::random(55)+1, Ns),
       N2 <> N1,
       N3 = tryGetNth(math::random(55)+1, Ns),
       N3 <> N2, N3 <> N1,
       N4 = tryGetNth(math::random(55)+1, Ns),
       N4 <> N3, N4 <> N2, N4 <> N1,
       N5 = tryGetNth(math::random(55)+1, Ns),
       N5 <> N4, N5 <> N3, N5 <> N2, N5 <> N1,
       RN = [N1, N2, N3, N4, N5],
       RMB = [tryGetNth(math::random(45)+1, MBs)],
       convertListToString(RN, RMB, S),
       assert(randomLotto1(S)),
       retract(regularNumbers(_)),
       retract(moneyBallNumbers(_)), !.
    get_Random():- get_Random().

    randomAgain(RL, R):-
       retract(leastCalledRandom(_)),
       retract(randomLotto1(_)),
       getHistoryData(LCN, LCMB, _, _, _, _, _, _),
```

# REFERENCES

```
        get_Random_LCN(LCN, LCMB),
        get_Random(),
        leastCalledRandom(RL),
        randomLotto1(R),!.
    randomAgain("","") :- !.

    displayHelp(Help):-
        HelpStr = file::readString(lottoHelpFile, IsUnicode),
        Help = concat("---------------Data Import and Massaging
    Instructions------------------\n\n", HelpStr),
        stdio::write(Help), !.

% ---------- Alternative method of getting the Help information line by line
% ---------------
%     displayHelp(Help):-
%     assert(helpString(" ------------ Data Import and Massaging
%     Instructions --------------\n\n")),
%     I = inputStream_file::openFile8(lottoHelpFile),
%     getHelp(I),
%     retract(helpString(Help)), !.
%     displayHelp(Help):-
%     Help = "Couldn't Find it ... \n\n", !.

%     getHelp(I) :-
%     not(I:endOfStream()),
%     InstructionLine = I:readLine(),
%     H2 = concat(InstructionLine,"\n"),
%     helpString(H1),
%     Help = concat(H1, H2),
%     retract(helpString(_)),
%     assert(helpString(Help)),
%     getHelp(I), !.
%     getHelp( ):-!.

    historyDataConvert(LCN, LCMB, MCN, MCMB, OCN, OCMB) :-
        convertListToString(LCN, LCMB, S1),
        convertListToString(MCN, MCMB, S2),
        convertListToString(OCN, OCMB, S3),
        assertz(leastCalledNumbers(S1)),
        assertz(mostCalledNumbers(S2)),
        assertz(oldestCalledNumbers(S3)),
        file::save(lottoNumbers, displayNumbers), !.
```

### A GUIDE TO ARTIFICIAL INTELLIGENCE WITH VISUAL PROLOG

```
convertListToString([N1, N2, N3, N4, N5 | _], [MB | _], String) :-
   S1 = concat(toString(N1), ", "),
   S2 = concat(toString(N2), ", "),
   S3 = concat(toString(N3), ", "),
   S4 = concat(toString(N4), ", "),
   S5 = concat(toString(N5), " "),
   S6 = concat("- ", toString(MB)),
   String = concat(S1, S2, S3, S4, S5, S6), !.

saveHistory():-
   file::existFile(lottoNumbers),
   file::delete(lottoNumbers),
   file::save(lottoNumbers, displayNumbers),
   retract(leastCalledNumbers(_)),
   retract(mostCalledNumbers(_)),
   retract(oldestCalledNumbers(_)),
   retract(leastCalledRandom(_)),
   retract(randomLotto1(_)),!.

saveHistory():-
   file::save(lottoNumbers, displayNumbers),
   retract(leastCalledNumbers(_)),
   retract(mostCalledNumbers(_)),
   retract(oldestCalledNumbers(_)),
   retract(leastCalledRandom(_)),
   retract(randomLotto1(_)),!.

saveHistory():- !.

clauses
   classInfo(className, classVersion).

end implement getNumbers
```

## 4.4.7 Numbers.cl

```
class numbers : numbers
   open core

predicates
   classInfo : core::classInfo.
   % @short Class information  predicate.
   % @detail This predicate represents information predicate of this class.
```

```
  % @end

predicates
  display : (window Parent) -> numbers Numbers.

constructors
  new : (window Parent).

end class numbers
```

## 4.4.8 Numbers.i

```
interface numbers supports formWindow
  open core

predicates
  set_form_text_for_LCN:(string).
  set_form_text_for_MCN:(string).
  set_form_text_for_OCN:(string).
  set_form_text_for_RLCN:(string).
  set_form_text_for_RAN:(string).

end interface numbers
```

## 4.4.9 Numbers.pro

```
implement numbers
  inherits formWindow
  open core, vpiDomains

constants
  className = "Lotto/numbers".
  classVersion = "".

clauses
  classInfo(className, classVersion).

clauses
  display(Parent) = Form :-
    Form = new(Parent),
    Form:show().
```

```
clauses
    new(Parent):-
        formWindow::new(Parent),
        generatedInitialize().

clauses
    set_form_text_for_LCN(L):-
        staticText1_ctl:setText(L),
        update().                               %to repaint

    set_form_text_for_MCN(M):-
        staticText3_ctl:setText(M),
        update().                               %to repaint

    set_form_text_for_OCN(O):-
        staticText5_ctl:setText(O),
        update().                               %to repaint

    set_form_text_for_RLCN(RLCN):-
        staticText7_ctl:setText(RLCN),
        update().                               %to repaint

    set_form_text_for_RAN(R):-
        staticText9_ctl:setText(R),
        update().                               %to repaint

predicates
    onSaveClick : button::clickResponder.
clauses
    onSaveClick(_Source) = button::defaultAction:-
        getNumbers::saveHistory().

predicates
    onAgainClick : button::clickResponder.
clauses
    onAgainClick(_Source) = button::noAction:-
        getNumbers::randomAgain(RL, R),
        staticText7_ctl:setText(RL),
        staticText9_ctl:setText(R),
        update().

% This code is maintained automatically, do not update it manually.
% 14:46:20-26.7.2009
facts
```

# REFERENCES

```
    again_ctl : button.
    save_ctl : button.
    staticText1_ctl : textControl.
    staticText3_ctl : textControl.
    staticText5_ctl : textControl.
    staticText7_ctl : textControl.
    staticText9_ctl : textControl.
predicates
    generatedInitialize : ().
clauses
    generatedInitialize():-
       setFont(vpi::fontCreateByName("Tahoma", 8)),
       setText("Numbers"),
       setRect(rct(50,40,282,160)),
       setDecoration(titlebar([closebutton()])),
       setBorder(sizeBorder()),
       setState([wsf_ClipSiblings,wsf_ClipChildren]),
       menuSet(resMenu(resourceIdentifiers::id_TaskMenu)),
       addShowListener(generatedOnShow),
       again_ctl := button::newOk(This),
       again_ctl:setText("&Again"),
       again_ctl:setPosition(56, 98),
       again_ctl:setAnchors([control::right,control::bottom]),
       again_ctl:setClickResponder(onAgainClick),
       save_ctl := button::newCancel(This),
       save_ctl:setText("&Save"),
       save_ctl:setPosition(128, 98),
       save_ctl:setAnchors([control::right,control::bottom]),
       save_ctl:setClickResponder(onSaveClick),
       StaticText_ctl = textControl::new(This),
       StaticText_ctl:setText("Least Called Numbers: "),
       StaticText_ctl:setPosition(36, 12),
       StaticText_ctl:setSize(80, 10),
       staticText1_ctl := textControl::new(This),
       staticText1_ctl:setText("Static text"),
       staticText1_ctl:setPosition(116, 12),
       staticText1_ctl:setSize(80, 10),
       StaticText2_ctl = textControl::new(This),
       StaticText2_ctl:setText("Most Called Numbers: "),
       StaticText2_ctl:setPosition(36, 28),
       StaticText2_ctl:setSize(80, 10),
       staticText3_ctl := textControl::new(This),
       staticText3_ctl:setText("Static text"),
```

## A GUIDE TO ARTIFICIAL INTELLIGENCE WITH VISUAL PROLOG

```
            staticText3_ctl:setPosition(116, 28),
            staticText3_ctl:setSize(80, 10),
            StaticText4_ctl = textControl::new(This),
            StaticText4_ctl:setText("Oldest Called Numbers: "),
            StaticText4_ctl:setPosition(36, 44),
            StaticText4_ctl:setSize(80, 10),
            staticText5_ctl := textControl::new(This),
            staticText5_ctl:setText("Static text"),
            staticText5_ctl:setPosition(116, 44),
            staticText5_ctl:setSize(80, 10),
            StaticText6_ctl = textControl::new(This),
            StaticText6_ctl:setText("Random Least Called: "),
            StaticText6_ctl:setPosition(36, 60),
            StaticText6_ctl:setSize(80, 10),
            staticText7_ctl := textControl::new(This),
            staticText7_ctl:setText("Static text"),
            staticText7_ctl:setPosition(116, 60),
            staticText7_ctl:setSize(80, 10),
            StaticText8_ctl = textControl::new(This),
            StaticText8_ctl:setText("Random1: "),
            StaticText8_ctl:setPosition(36, 76),
            StaticText8_ctl:setSize(80, 10),
            staticText9_ctl := textControl::new(This),
            staticText9_ctl:setText("Static text"),
            staticText9_ctl:setPosition(116, 76),
            staticText9_ctl:setSize(80, 10).

    predicates
        generatedOnShow: window::showListener.
    clauses
        generatedOnShow(_,_):-
            succeed.
% end of automatic code
end implement numbers
```

## 4.4.10 Help.cl

```
    class help : help
        open core

    predicates
        classInfo : core::classInfo.
        % @short Class information  predicate.
```

## REFERENCES

```
    % @detail This predicate represents information predicate of this class.
    % @end

predicates
    display : (window Parent) -> help Help.

constructors
    new : (window Parent).

end class help
```

## 4.4.11 Help.i

```
interface help supports formWindow
    open core

predicates
    set_form_text:(string).

end interface help
```

## 4.4.12 Help.pro

```
implement help
    inherits formWindow
    open core, vpiDomains

constants
    className = "Lotto/help".
    classVersion = "".

clauses
    classInfo(className, classVersion).

clauses
    display(Parent) = Form :-
        Form = new(Parent),
        Form:show().

clauses
    new(Parent):-
        formWindow::new(Parent),
```

## A GUIDE TO ARTIFICIAL INTELLIGENCE WITH VISUAL PROLOG

```
        generatedInitialize().

    clauses
      set_form_text(Help):-
        staticText_ctl:setForegroundColor(color_Blue ),
        staticText_ctl:setText(Help),
        update().                              %to repaint

  % This code is maintained automatically, do not update it manually.
  % 14:24:39-15.8.2009
  facts
      staticText_ctl : textControl.

  predicates
      generatedInitialize : ().
  clauses
      generatedInitialize():-
        setFont(vpi::fontCreateByName("Tahoma", 8)),
        setText("Help"),
        setRect(rct(50,40,458,374)),
        setDecoration(titlebar([closebutton(), maximizebutton(),minimizebutton()])),
        setBorder(sizeBorder()),
        setState([wsf_ClipSiblings,wsf_ClipChildren]),
        menuSet(noMenu),
        addShowListener(generatedOnShow),
        staticText_ctl := textControl::new(This),
        staticText_ctl:setText("Static text"),
        staticText_ctl:setPosition(4, 2),
        staticText_ctl:setSize(400, 330).

  predicates
      generatedOnShow: window::showListener.
  clauses
      generatedOnShow(_,_):-
        succeed.
  % end of automatic code
  end implement help
```

## 4.4.13 HelpWindow.cl

```
    class helpWindow : window
      open core
```

predicates
    classInfo : core::classInfo.
    % @short Class information  predicate.
    % @detail This predicate represents information predicate of this class.
    % @end

constructors
    new : (window Parent, string Filename).

end class helpWindow

## 4.4.14 HelpWindow.pro

    implement helpWindow
    inherits documentwindow
        open core, lottoDomains, vpidomains, resourceidentifiers

constants
    className = "Lotto/helpWindow".
    classVersion = "".

    windowFlags : vpiDomains::wsflags = [wsf_SizeBorder, wsf_TitleBar, wsf_Maximize, wsf_Minimize, wsf_Close, wsf_ClipSiblings, wsf_ClipChildren].
    rectangle : vpiDomains::rct = rct(100, 80, 752, 462).
    menu : vpiDomains::menu = resMenu(id_TaskMenu).

clauses
    classInfo(className, classVersion).

facts
    filename : string.
    parent : window.
    isUnicode : boolean.

clauses
  new(Parent, FileName) :-
    documentWindow::new(Parent),
    filename := FileName,
    parent := Parent,
    isUnicode := false.

 class predicates

# A GUIDE TO ARTIFICIAL INTELLIGENCE WITH VISUAL PROLOG

```
        getFileContent : (
         string Filename,
         string InputStr,
         boolean IsUnicode) determ (i,o,o).

    clauses
        getFileContent("", "", true) :- !.
        getFileContent(FileName, InputStr, IsUnicode) :-
        InputStr = file::readString(FileName, IsUnicode).

        show():-
        getFileContent(filename, InputStr, IsUnicode), !,
        ReadOnly = b_false,
        Indent = b_true,
        InitPos = 1,
        isUnicode := IsUnicode,
        Font = vpi::fontCreate(ff_fixed, [], 8),
        HWND = vpiEditor::create(w_toplevel, rectangle, "", menu,
        parent:getvpiwindow(),
            windowFlags, Font, ReadOnly,
            Indent, InputStr, InitPos, geteventHandler()),
            vpi::winSetFont(HWND, Font).
        show():-
            vpiCommonDialogs::note(string::format(
            "File <%s> does not exist", filename)).

    end implement helpWindow
```

## 4.4.15 TaskWindow.pro

```
    implement taskWindow
        inherits applicationWindow
        open core, vpiDomains, lottoDomains

    constants
        className = "TaskWindow/taskWindow".
        classVersion = "".

    clauses
        classInfo(className, classVersion).

    constants
        mdiProperty : boolean = true.
```

# REFERENCES

```
clauses
  new():-
    applicationWindow::new(),
    generatedInitialize().

predicates
  onShow : window::showListener.
clauses
  onShow(_, _CreationData):-
    _MessageForm = messageForm::display(This).

predicates
  onDestroy : window::destroyListener.
clauses
  onDestroy(_).


predicates
  onHelpAbout : window::menuItemListener.
clauses
  onHelpAbout(TaskWin, _MenuTag):-
    _AboutDialog = aboutDialog::display(TaskWin).
predicates
  onFileExit : window::menuItemListener.

clauses
  onFileExit(_, _MenuTag):-
    close().

predicates
  onSizeChanged : window::sizeListener.
clauses
  onSizeChanged( ):-
    vpiToolbar::resize(getVPIWindow()).

predicates
  onImportData : window::menuItemListener.
clauses
  onImportData(_Source, _MenuTag) :-
    convertData::getData().

predicates
  onGetNumbers : window::menuItemListener.
clauses
```

### A GUIDE TO ARTIFICIAL INTELLIGENCE WITH VISUAL PROLOG

```
    onGetNumbers(_Source, _MenuTag) :-
      Form = numbers::new(This),
      Form:show(),
      getNumbers::history([L, M, O, RL, R]),
      Form:set_form_text_for_LCN(L),
      Form:set_form_text_for_MCN(M),
      Form:set_form_text_for_OCN(O),
      Form:set_form_text_for_RLCN(RL),
      Form:set_form_text_for_RAN(R), !.

predicates
    onHelpDownloadProcedure : window::menuItemListener.
clauses
    onHelpDownloadProcedure(Source, _MenuTag):-
      Form2 = help::new(This),
      Form2:show(),
      getNumbers::displayHelp(Help),
      Form2:set_form_text(Help),
      HelpWindow = helpWindow::new(Source, lottoHelpFile),
      HelpWindow:show().

% This code is maintained automatically, do not update it manually.
% 15:17:21-26.7.2009
predicates
    generatedInitialize : ().
clauses
    generatedInitialize():-
      setText("LottoTest"),
      setDecoration(titlebar([closebutton(), maximizebutton(),minimizebutton()])),
      setBorder(sizeBorder()),
      setState([wsf_ClipSiblings]),
      setMdiProperty(mdiProperty),
      menuSet(resMenu(resourceIdentifiers::id_TaskMenu)),
      addShowListener(generatedOnShow),
      addShowListener(onShow),
      addSizeListener(onSizeChanged),
      addDestroyListener(onDestroy),
      addMenuItemListener(resourceIdentifiers::id_help_about, onHelpAbout),
      addMenuItemListener(resourceIdentifiers::id_file_exit, onFileExit),
      addMenuItemListener(resourceIdentifiers::id_import_data,
        onImportData),
      addMenuItemListener(resourceIdentifiers::id_get_numbers,
        onGetNumbers),
      addMenuItemListener(resourceIdentifiers::
```

# REFERENCES

```
        id_help_download_procedure, onHelpDownloadProcedure).

predicates
    generatedOnShow: window::showListener.
clauses
    generatedOnShow(_,_):-
        projectToolbar::create(getVPIWindow()),
        statusLine::create(getVPIWindow()),
        succeed.

% end of automatic code
end implement taskWindow
```

## 4.4.16 ImportInstructions.hlp

To Convert Downloaded Georgia Mega Lotto numbers for Program use, do the following:

1. Download the number history from
    "http://www.galottery.com/stc/games/megaMillions.jsp"

    They will be in a file named "MegaMillionsHistroy.cvs"; and, should look as follows when opened in a spreadsheet application (such as Excel):

    Draw Date "Draw Result"
    1/6/2009    03-11-12-19-33  MB=30
    1/2/2009    02-11-19-21-34  MB=38
    12/30/2008  01-22-29-44-52  MB=39
    12/26/2008  06-19-29-33-37  MB=31
    and so on....

2. Using Excel [or whatever Spreadsheet Application you use] do the following:

    a. Modify the data by deleting the Rows predeeding the Rows with Numbers
    b. Use the "Save as" feature to Save It as a "*.txt" type file under the name of "Stats.txt", which is readable with Microsoft Notepad

3. Because Notepad can not find and replace non-printable characters like Tabs, and Carraige Returns, use a word processing application like Microsoft Word which can, to make the following modifications to the "Stats.txt" using the "Find and Replace All" feature:

a. Replace all Tabs with a " " [i.e. replace all Tabs with a Space Character]
b. Replace all "/" with " " [i.e. replace Slashes with a Space Character]
c. Replace all "-" with " " [i.e. replace all Hyphens with a Space Character]
d. Replace all " MB=" with "" [i.e. replace all " MB=" characters with Nothing]
e. Use the Save feature to save it.

Important - When saving it, keep it in the ".txt" format as Word Processing applictions will insert other assorted information that will cause problems for this Lotto program.

4. When you are done, the file should now look as follows and be usable by this Lotto Program under the "Import Data" Option (and be viewable in Notepad as well if you wish - a simpler application to use, however no more editing should be required):

1 6 2009 03 11 12 19 33 30
1 2 2009 02 11 19 21 34 38
12 30 2008 01 22 29 44 52 39
12 26 2008 06 19 29 33 37 31
and so on….

5. Notes:

a. In the "Stats.txt" file, the data should now only have 9 number groups per row, with each number separated by a single space character, with the following meaning for each number group:

Month, Day, Year, 5 Regular Numbers, and the Money Ball Number

b. There should be no other information preceding this data or following it.

c. If you have problems, you may wish to look for un-needed non-printable characters like Tabs, Carriage Returns, etc; or, maybe double spaces They will cause problems.